Talking Points on Global Issues
A Reader

Richard H. Robbins
SUNY at Plattsburgh

Boston   New York   San Francisco
Mexico City   Montreal   Toronto   London   Madrid   Munich   Paris
Hong Kong   Singapore   Tokyo   Cape Town   Sydney

Copyright © 2004 Pearson Education, Inc.

All rights reserved. No part of the material protected by this copyright notice may be reproduced or utilized in any form or by any means, electronic or mechanical, including photocopying, recording, or by any information storage and retrieval system, without written permission from the copyright owner.

To obtain permission(s) to use material from this work, please submit a written request to Allyn and Bacon, Permissions Department, 75 Arlington Street, Boston, MA 02116 or fax your request to 617-848-7320.

ISBN   0-205-41925-9

Printed in the United States of America

10 9 8 7 6 5 4 3 2 1   08 07 06 05 04 03

Table of Contents

Talking Points on Global Problems

V Reading Set Number Five: Population

1. U.S. Eugenics Like Nazi Policy Study: Forced Sterilizations Carried Out Longer Than Thought by David Morgan (Reuters, February 14, 2000)

2. Peru Apologizes For At Least 200,000 Forced Sterilizations (United Press International July 25, 2002)

VI Reading Set Number Six: Poverty, Hunger, and Economic Development

1. Global Poverty: The Gap Between the World's Rich and Poor Is Growing, and the Dying Continues by Thomas W. Pogge (Public Affairs Report. Vol. 42, No. 2, Summer 2001)

2. Global Falsehoods: How the World Bank and the UNDP Distort the Figures on Global Poverty by Michel Chossudovsky

VII Reading Set Number Seven: The Environment

1. The Environmentalists Are Wrong By Bjorn Lomborg (*New York Times*, August 26, 2002)

2. Corporations Urged Not To 'Appease' Environmental Groups By Marc Morano (CNSNews.com February 03, 2003)

3. Environmental Trends. By Peter Montague. (*Rachel's Environment and Health News*, #737 November 8, 2001)

VIII Reading Set Number Eight: Health and Disease

1. Southern Sickness, Northern Medicine: Patently Wrong by Philippe Riviere (*Le Monde Diplomatique*, July 2001)

2. 2 Paths of Bayer Drug in 80's: Riskier Type Went Overseas By Walt Bogdanich and Eric Koli (*New York Times*, May 22, 2003)

IX Reading Set Number Nine: Indigenous Peoples

1. The Pressure to Modernize and Globalize by Helena Norberg-Hodge (from *The Case Against the Global Economy – And a Turn Toward the Local*, edited by Jerry Mander and Edward Goldsmith, Sierra Club Books, 1996)

2. In the Native Way by Tom Goldtooth (Reprinted from *Yes! A Journal of Positive Futures*, Winter 2002)

X Reading Set Number Ten: Peasant Protest

1. Farm Unrest Roils Mexico, Challenging New President by Ginger Thompson (*New York Times*, July 22, 2001)

2. The New Peasant's Revolt by Katherine Ainger (*New Internationalist Magazine*, #353, January-February 2003)

XI Reading Set Number Eleven: Antisystemic Protest

1. Who are the Global Terrorists? *by Noam Chomsky (*Reprinted from Ken Booth and Tim Dunne eds., *Worlds in Collision: Terror and the Future of Global Order*, Palgrave/Macmillan, UK, May 2002)

2. Euro Law Wrongly Defines Terrorism by John Brown. (*Le Monde Diplomatique*, February 2002

XII Reading Set Number Twelve: Religious Protest

1. On a String and a Prayer: In nation after nation religion has taken on a role as the primary force for political change, by Mark I. Pinsky *(The Orlando Sentinel*, December 14, 1997)

2. Does religion promote—or subvert—civil society? By Timothy A. Brown *Civnet Journal*, january–february 1999 • vol 3. no. 1

Reading Set Thirteen: The Citizen-Activist

1. Reading Number 1: The Growth Consensus Unravels by Jonathan Rowe (*Dollars and Sense: The Magazine of Economic Justice*: Issue #224, July-August 1999)

2. The Prosperous Community : Social Capital and Public Life by Robert Putnam (*American Prospect* Vol 4, no 13, March 21, 1993)

Introduction

Talking Points on Global Problems is designed to promote discussion and thought on global issues that have a direct bearing on our everyday lives. The reader is organized into 13 problems that correspond to the chapters in *Global Problems and the Culture of Capitalism*, although the reader is designed be used independently.

The readings vary from brief newspaper articles to studies on global economic conditions, to excerpts from books. In some cases sets of readings have been selected to present different views of issues (e.g. are human beings "naturally materialistic or do they have to be taught to consume?), while in others to highlight specific problems (e.g. how does one define terrorism?) In all cases the readings have been selected to provoke discussion by offering perspectives on global problems that require thinking through or talking about policies, events, and ideas that affect all of us.

Each set of readings is accompanied by exercises and study questions. These can be used as class discussion topics, or as guides to the readings. To the extent that learning and insight are best achieved by "talking things out," it is furthered also by "writing things out."

The field of cultural anthropology has often been characterized as cultural critique; that is, it is a discipline that, among other things, tries to develop a critical view of culture and society. The goal of the critique is not to present a necessarily negative view of a society, but, rather, to help foster an understanding of how and why a society functions. Through critique and the understanding that it fosters, it becomes possible to work through and solve problems that inevitably arise in the collective effort to build meaning and order. This reader has been prepared in that spirit.

Reading Set One: The Consumer

Problem: Has the desire in capitalist society to consume ever greater quantities of goods a culturally or socially constructed desire, or is it part of human nature to want to accumulate stuff?

Exercise: Suppose we set as public policy the promotion of a simpler, less materialistic way of life. What might some of the positive and negative consequences of such as policy be.

The culture of capitalism requires constant feeding by consumers. That is, unless people buy more this year than last and more next year than this, the economy, on which our culture is built, would collapse. It was no accident that the day after two planes crashed into the World Trade Center in New York City, political leaders urged the public to resume their normal life and "shop and work."

In the culture of capitalism, we are all consumers. It was not always this way. In past centuries, except for a small elite who demonstrated their status through the conspicuous display of material things, most people saw virtue in thrift and modesty. In some cases the conspicuous display of wealth was prohibited to all but a very few. That began to change in the United States and Europe in the late nineteenth and early twentieth century when government and business began to urge people to consume even greater quantities of goods.

All of this poses a significant issue; to what extent is the vociferous consumption evident today a function of some sort of natural urge to take pleasure in material things, or to what extent is it a function of our culture? Do we consume naturally, or is it, as some believe, a carefully and even cynically nurtured behavior?

Is it, as Ignacio Ramonet asks, a "cultural and social construction"?

In his article, Ramonet portrays the efforts of advertisers to manufacture desire, the tricks used to persuade people to buy. Others, such as James B. Twitchell, depict mass consumption as a triumph; Twitchell sees the triumph of consumption as a consequence of the simple fact that "human beings love things." Commercialism, he says, is not forcing us to do something that we wouldn't do anyway. Getting and spending is what gives our life order and meaning. It makes us happy, even serving as a replacement for spiritual fulfillment.

Finally, in his article Alan Thein Durning takes issue with Twitchell's thesis. Consumption, Durning says, does not make us happy; if it did, we wouldn't constantly desire more and more stuff. We are no happier now than we were consuming half of what we do now.

Study Questions

1. What are the implicit promises made about products by advertisers? How much of their message is retained?

2. How does advertising deflect criticism of itself?

3. According to Twitchell what is the origin of the urge to consume? How does it relate to spiritual things?

4. How is democracy related to consumption?

5. Why, according to Durning, does increased consumption fail to make us any happier?

6. What, according to Durning, are the real determinants of happiness?

Reading Number 1. Manufacturing Desire

by Ignacio Ramonet (Le Monde Diplomatique, May 2001)

"The trade of advertising is now so near perfection that it is not easy to propose any improvement." Samuel Johnson, 1759.

Advertising and its tricks are not new. As early as the 12th century town criers ran through the streets shouting out announcements. In the 18th century, with the introduction of lithography, the first commercial advertisements appeared and covered all available walls and fences. In the 19th century advertising became a market-centered activity, creating the publicity machine as it conquered the newspapers.

"In 1836 Emile de Girardin decided to launch his mass circulation daily newspaper La Presse and to make space available for commercial advertising," says Libération. "In 1832 Charles Havas set up the first international information agency, which was soon dealing with advertising as well. In 1865 classified ads accounted for one-third of newspaper space". In the late 19th century the large companies founded during the industrial revolution began creating mass markets and shaping demand. For there is nothing "natural" about mass consumption. It is a cultural and social construction.

In 1892 Coca-Cola already had one of the world's largest advertising budgets. In 1912 the Advertising Club of America declared it to be the best-publicized American product Coca-Cola's advertising budget for that year included $300,000 for newspaper ads, a million calendars, 2m ashtrays, 5m lithographic signs and 10m Coca-Cola-colored matchboxes. The company's executives had understood that they had to reach the largest number of potential buyers. As one put it, "Repetition wins out in the end. One drop of water can pierce a rock".

With the rise of the media electric (cinema and radio), electronic (television) and digital (internet) advertising, of increasing sophistication, expanded enormously in the 20th century. The drive to shape people's thinking and reach into their homes achieved semi-scientific status. Techniques of persuasion became refined enough to pierce the constant hubbub of communication and deliver precise messages to our brains.

The advertising barrage in developed nations is now estimated at a total of 2,500 daily hits per person. In 1999 the French TV channels showed more than 500,000 ads. These sorts of figures mean that any single commercial has very little chance of standing out. One study found that 85% of ads had no effect at all on their intended audience, 5% had a negative effect (they "boomeranged") and only 10% had any positive influence. Moreover, due to the imperfections of human memory, the 10% figure dips to only 5% after 24 hours: 95% of all ads are lost.

In the blinking of an eye

What must advertising do to influence us? There was an attempt to reduce messages to a single image subliminal imagery to make advertising imperceptible. A "parasite" image inserted within the 24 frames per second used in the cinema (25 per second on TV) circumvents normal retinal reaction time. The eye sees the message and the brain registers it, but only subliminally, below the edge of consciousness (from the Latin limen, threshold).

This is regarded as illegal, but the idea still appeals. In France, following François Mitterrand's 1988 election victory, the newspaper Le Quotidien de Paris accused him of having benefited from secret "subliminal images" hidden in the credits of a TV news program aired on the Antenne 2 network. Legal proceedings were brought on the grounds of electoral manipulation but the plaintiffs were unsuccessful. France's regulatory body for telecommunications and broadcasting nevertheless decided to ban all hidden images.

Last May an American group accused the film Battlefield Earth, based on a novel by L Ron Hubbard, founder of Scientology, of "containing subliminal images" designed to win converts. Last September, in the middle of the United States election campaign, George W Bush acknowledged that an ad produced by his Republican team contained a subliminal image. The ad was critical of the platform of his Democratic opponent, Al Gore. Superimposed over Gore's picture was the phrase "The Gore Prescription Plan:

Bureaucrats Decide." Then, over a black background, the last four letters of the word "bureaucrats" appeared in capitals RATS for a fraction of a second, filling the entire screen. Under intense media pressure, the Bush campaign was forced to pull the ad.

Advertising sees itself as the art of persuasion, and its messages are carefully wrought. Consumers and their visual reactions are studied in depth. Prior to distribution, images are sometimes tested using an eye camera spectators watch an image and their pupil response is recorded by an invisible camera. The path traced by the eye can be statistically determined: what the eye sees first, what it fails to see. This test is the result of research and collaboration between specialists, including sociologists, psychologists, semioticians, linguists, graphic designers, decorators.

Such a confluence of expertise made Marshall McLuhan conclude that:

"No group of sociologists can approximate the ad teams in the gathering and processing of exploitable social data. The ad teams have billions of dollars to spend annually on research and testing of reactions, and their products are magnificent accumulations of material about the shared experience and feelings of the entire community".

Children are a favorite target audience. France's Syndicat national de la publicité télévisée estimates that advertisers in France spent more than $140m in 1999 on advertisements aimed at children under 14. The Institut de l'enfant estimates that approximately 45% of French families' spending ($70bn a year) is directly influenced by children's desires. "The opinions of kids between four and 10 have a major influence on purchases of food, sweets, textiles and toys," says Joël-Yves Le Bigot, the institute's director, "but they also influence 18% of automobile purchases and 40% of decisions relating to holiday destinations".

Paper moon

Advertising always promises the same things well being, comfort, effectiveness, happiness and success and delivers assurances of future satisfaction. Advertising deals in dreams, pointing out pathways to trouble-free social ascent. Advertising constructs desire and shows a world on perpetual holiday, relaxed, smiling, carefree. A world filled with happy people clutching the miracle product that will make them feel beautiful, clean, fit, free, attractive, fashionable.

Advertising sells everything to everybody without discrimination, as if mass society were class-free. In the view of semiotician Louis Quesnel, "In the face of a harrowing world, which TV shows us all, advertising evokes a vision of a utopia cleansed of tragedy, a world without under-developed countries, nuclear weapons, overpopulation or wars. A world of innocence, full of light and smiles, optimistic, heavenly".

By the power of repetition, ads lend credence to the great myths of our time: modernity, youth, happiness, leisure, prosperity. Women are confined in a system that mostly recognizes them only as sexual or domestic objects. They feel guilty, under relentless surveillance, accountable when their home and laundry are less than spotless, when their skin and body start to decline. They are answerable for their children's health and hygiene, the state of their husband's stomach, their household's finances. At the office, in the kitchen, on the beach, in the shower, women are still dependent. Men will judge them whatever they do. Even if a woman gets freedom through work, men will still scrutinize the shade of her suntan, the smell of her armpits, the shininess of her hair, the freshness of her breath, the shapeliness of her bosom and the color of her tights.

William Zimmermann, the former anti-Vietnam war activist, believes that there is no shame in using advertising to get one's message across: "Today the progressive class in America has no choice: either be destroyed by the system or, as we have now come to understand, destroy the system with its own weapons" . But the situation is not quite that simple, since advertising's goal is to recycle everything. Symbols like the hammer and sickle (as in ads for Self-Trade, the European e-broking group) and revolutionary figures such as Marx (used by UFF, the leading French bank), Lenin (in ads for Liberty Surf, the French internet service provider), Mao (UFF), Zapata (Liberty Surf) and Che Guevara (Liberty Surf), have all served as foils for the internet "revolution".

Frédéric Beigbeder writes: "In the past dictatorships feared freedom of expression, censored political opposition, locked up writers and burned controversial books. In order to subjugate humanity, advertising has kept a low profile, preferring flexibility and persuasion instead. For the first time we are living within a system of human domination against which even freedom is powerless. Indeed the system stakes all it has on liberty, and this is its masterstroke. Any criticism works to the system's own advantage, and anti-advertising diatribes only reinforce the illusion of its sweetly smiling tolerance. The system obtains one's submission with elegance. It has achieved its goal since disobedience itself has become a form of obedience".

As a structurally reductionist force, advertising offers a compressed and oversimplified view of the world. It relies on stereotypes to dictate our desires. Worst of all, it forces us to accept our own enslavement.

Reading Number 2: A (Mild) Defense of Luxury By JAMES B. TWITCHELL (From Living It Up: Our Love Affair With Luxury. Colombia University Press, 2002; also reprinted in The Chronicle of Higher Education March 15, 2002)

Who but fools, toadies, and hacks have ever come to the defense of modern American luxury? No one, not even bulk consumers of the stuff, will ever really defend it. And why should they? The very idea that what we have defines who we are is repulsive to many of us. The irrationality of overvaluing certain rocks, fabrics, logos, textures, wines, bottles, appliances, nameplates, tassels, ZIP codes, T-shirts, monograms, hotel rooms, purses, and the like is insulting to our intellect. At one level this kind of luxury is indefensible. The "good life" seems so blatantly unnecessary, even evil, especially when millions of people around the globe are living without the bare necessities.

Generations ago the market for luxury goods consisted of a few people who lived in majestic houses with a full complement of servants, in some time-honored enclave of the privileged. As Holly Brubach has wittily observed, they ordered their trunks from Louis Vuitton, their trousseaux from Christian Dior, their Dom Perignon by the case, and spent lots of time looking out over water. Their taste, like their politics, was determined largely by considerations of safeguarding wealth and perpetuating the social conventions that affirmed their sense of superiority. They stayed put. We watched them from afar. We stayed put. Maybe they had money to burn. We had to buy coal.

The very unassailability of old luxe made it safe, like old name, old blood, old land, old pew, old coat of arms, or old service to the crown. Primogeniture, the cautious passage and consolidation of wealth to the first-born male, made the anxiety of exclusion somehow bearable. After all, you knew your place from the moment of birth and had plenty of time to make your peace. If you drew a short straw, not to worry. A comfortable life as a vicar would await you. Or the officer corps. For females marriage became the defining act of social place.

The application of steam, and then electricity, to the engines of production brought a new market of status, an industrial market, one made up of people who essentially had bought their way into having a blood line. These were the people who so disturbed Veblen, and from them this new generation of consumer has descended. First the industrial rich, then the inherited rich, and now the incidentally rich, the accidentally rich. Call them yuppies, yippies, bobos, nobrows, or whatever; although they can't afford a house in Paris's 16th Arrondissement or an apartment on Park Avenue, they have enough disposable income to buy a Vuitton handbag (if not a trunk), a bottle of Dior perfume (if not a flagon), a Bombay martini (if not quite a few), and a time-share vacation on the water (if not a second home). The consumers of the new luxury have a sense of entitlement that transcends social class, a conviction that the finer things are their birthright—never mind that they were born into a family whose estate is a tract house in the suburbs, near the mall, still not paid for, and whose family crest comes downloaded from the Internet.

These new customers for luxury are younger than clients of the old luxe used to be, they are far more numerous, they make their money far sooner, and they are far more flexible in financing and fickle in choice. They do not stay put. They now have money to burn. The competition for their attention is intense, and their consumption patterns—if you haven't noticed—are changing life for the rest of us. They seem almost recession-proof. How concerned should we be? I say, not very. Let them eat cake.

Now, mind you, luxury has nothing to do with happiness. As Freud famously said of consuming another product— psychotherapy—high-end consumption will not make you happier, only less anxious. While the poor, loveless, ever-anxious crowd may think that individual satisfaction tracks closely with luxury consumption, such is not the case. Numerous studies show that as society grows richer over time, the average level of happiness—as measured by the percentage of people who rate themselves "happy" or "very happy" in national surveys—doesn't budge. In fact, sometimes it falls.

Does this mean consumption is a treadmill going nowhere? Well-tenured and - tended economists like Robert Frank and Juliet Schor certainly argue that it does. But one might suggest that at least the treadmills get more comfortable and more people have more access to them. That's got to mean something.

Economists have known about this perplexity for a while. In a famous 1972 essay titled "Is Growth Obsolete?" the Yale University economists William Nordhaus and James Tobin pointed out that the growing gross domestic product doesn't account for such important factors as leisure, household labor, pollution, and unsnarling traffic jams. In fact, in many categories, quality of life may even decline as high-end consumption increases.

On the heels of this study, Richard Easterlin, now an economic historian at the University of Southern California, argued that there was no clear trend in surveys of Americans' reported happiness. Average happiness rose from the 1940s to the late 1950s, then gradually sank again until the early 1970s, even as personal income grew sharply. Returning to the subject a few years ago, Easterlin cited an annual U.S. survey that showed a slight downward trend in the percentage of Americans saying they were "very happy," from 1972 to 1991 -- even though per-capita income, adjusted for inflation and taxes, rose by a third. In fact, this perplexity has become so established that it is known as the "Easterlin paradox."

So let's forget any argument that happiness correlates with buying stuff, let alone luxurious stuff. Lottery winners don't stay happier than other people for long (about two weeks), and accident victims who become paraplegics typically return over time to pre-trauma levels. So if happiness is not related to consumption, why not tamp down luxury consumption by taxing it -- or shaming it—into oblivion?

The answer is not rocket science; in fact, it's simple. While being on the treadmill to the Land of Opuluxe may not provide happiness, not being on the treadmill almost certainly guarantees unhappiness. And discomfort. Instead of asking the haves how they are feeling, ask the have-nots. Their answer is existentially simple. Forget where we're going, and since there is nowhere else to go, why not get there in comfort? All aboard. Ironically, the problem is not how to get some people off the treadmill but how to get other people on. If goods are what carry meaning in this world (and, alas, they do, and have always), then the poor are doubly disenfranchised: They don't have stuff, and they don't have the meanings that stuff carries.

While the happiness-as-be-all-and-end-all argument has the whiff of a red herring, it is not entirely dismissible. Before you denounce (or applaud) happiness research as left-ist propaganda, be aware that it also cuts the other way. For example, if happiness doesn't equate with income, why worry about minimum wages or distributions to the poor? Or to move it up a notch, if you don't want a society in which everyone is desperately trying to get ahead, you might advocate government policies that slow down consumption: high tax rates, generous health and unemployment benefits, long mandatory paid vacations, maybe even a limit on individual working hours. In other words, you might want to turn the United States into France. But are the French happier? Nope. France has an unemployment rate more than twice as high as that of the United States, largely because of those same government policies. And unemployment makes some people very unhappy.

Professor Stanley Lebergott, an economist at Wesleyan University, has ventured into this moral and economic quicksand. A few years ago he argued in Pursuing Happiness:

American Consumers in the Twentieth Century that Americans have spent their way to happiness. Lest this sound overly Panglossian, what Lebergott means is that while consumption by the rich has remained relatively steady, the rest of us have certainly had a good go of it. If we think that the rich are different from you and me, and that the difference is that the rich have longer shopping lists, then we have, in the last 50 years, substantially caught up.

The most interesting part of Pursuing Happiness is the second half of the book. Here Lebergott unloads reams of government statistics and calculations to chart the path that American consumption has taken through a wide range of products and services—food, tobacco, clothing, fuel, domestic service, and medicine, to name only a few. Two themes emerge strongly from these data.

The first, not surprisingly, is that Americans were far better off in 1990 than they were in 1900. For example, real consumer spending rose in 70 of the 84 years from 1900 to 1984. In 1990 an hour's work earned six times as much as in 1900. Most Americans walked to work at the start of the century, but by 1990 relatively few did, in part because nearly 90 percent of families had a car. By 1987 all households had a fridge, a radio, onetime luxuries; nearly all had a TV; and about three-quarters had a washing machine. Per-capita spending on food rose by more than 75 percent from 1900 to 1990, with a marked increase in meat consumption. "Wants" became "necessities" because, ironically, the pushing and shoving of other consumers was lowering the price. Your consumption of luxury has made life easier for me.

The second theme emerging from Lebergott's data is that old-line, left-leaning academic critics such as Robert Heilbroner, Tibor Scitovsky, Robert and Helen

Lynd, and legions of others now teaching American studies, who have censured the waste and tastelessness of much of American consumerism, may have simply missed the big point. Ditto the Voluntary Simplifiers with all their self-help books, their how-to-buy-less magazines, and their cut-excess-consumption videos. OK, OK, money can't buy happiness, but you stand a better chance than with penury.

Lebergott poses a simple question for such critics: Would they want to return to 1900? Even if they say yes, in a democratic society would they be justified in forcing their aesthetic and moral judgments on other consumers? And if they say yes, they should carefully watch the recent BBC-PBS show called 1900 House. As a modern family found by trying it, life at the turn of the 20th century was hard, very hard indeed. The idea that it was easy is one of our most cherished luxuries.

While studies may show that people who purchase luxuries are not happier than those who cannot, they also show that being able to consume these positional objects seems to be a driving force in most large social groups today. Call these goods whatever you want—bridge goods, heraldic goods, demonstration goods—the ability to have them seems to be restructuring communities. Happiness may not be improved by having luxe, but unhappiness is increased by not being able to get into the supposed community of supposed peers.

It is now clear why modern transgenerational poverty is so debilitating. If who you are is increasingly what you have, then the have-nots are doubly distressed. For not only do the poor miss out on creature comforts; they miss out on community meanings. Whatever these meanings may be, they are superpotent and no longer culturally specific. No Berlin Wall can keep them out for long. This new definition of must-have luxury is spreading around the globe at the speed of first the television and now the Internet.

We need to be reminded that luxury has a bright side as well as a dark side. Yes, luxury is a one-dimensional marker of status and hierarchy. Yes, pecuniary emulation is still key for shallow social distinctions and contrived position. And, yes, such positional power is transitory. Opuluxe is one-dimensional, shallow, ahistorical, without memory, and expendable. But it is also strangely democratic and unifying. If what you want is peace on earth, a unifying system that transcends religious, cultural, and caste differences, well— whoops! -- here it is. The Global Village is not quite the City on the Hill, not quite the Emerald City, and certainly not quite what millennial utopians had in mind, but it is closer to the equitable distribution of rank than what other systems have provided.

Remember in King Lear when the two nasty daughters want to strip Lear of his remaining trappings of majesty? He has moved in with them, and they don't think he needs so many expensive guards. They convince themselves by saying that their dad, who is used to having everything he has ever wanted, doesn't need a hundred or even a dozen soldiers around him. They whittle away at his retinue until only one is left. "What needs one?" they say.

Rather like governments attempting to redistribute wealth or like academics criticizing the consumption habits of others, they conclude that his needs are excessive. They are false needs: sumptuous, wasteful, luxurious. Lear, however, knows otherwise. Terrified and suddenly bereft of purpose, he bellows from his innermost soul, "Reason not the need."

True, Lear doesn't need these soldiers any more than Scrooge needed silver, Midas needed gold, the characters on Friends need stuff from Crate and Barrel, those shoppers on Rodeo Drive, Worth Avenue, and Madison Avenue need handbags, or I need to spend the night at the Bellagio. But not needing doesn't stop the desiring. Lear knows that possessions are definitions—superficial meanings, perhaps, but meanings nonetheless. Without soldiers he is no king. Without a BMW there can be no yuppie, without tattoos no adolescent rebel, without big hair no Southwestern glamorpuss, without Volvos no academic intellectuals, without cake no Marie Antoinette.

Professor Robert Frank tells a revealing story in his Luxury Fever: Why Money Fails to Satisfy in an Era of Excess. It seems a relative of his bought a red Porsche in France. When the relative returned to California, he found that the German car couldn't be retrofitted to meet the state's rigorous pollution regulations. He offered it to the professor at a fraction of its market value. Now, in Professor Frank's words:

"I was sorely tempted. Yet my small upstate college town has a strong, if usually unstated, social norm against conspicuous consumption. People here are far more likely to drive Volvos than Jaguars, and although ours is a cold climate, we almost never see anyone wearing a fur coat. At that time, a red Porsche convertible really would have been seen as an in-your-face car in a community like ours. Although I have never thought of myself as someone unusually sensitive to social pressure, I realized that unless I could put a sign on the car that explained how I happened to acquire it, I would never really feel comfortable driving it."

Professor Frank knows exactly what goods to buy and exactly what goods not to buy. He doesn't want to keep up with the Joneses or ditch the Joneses. He wants to fit in with the Joneses. He knows who the Joneses are. It's pretty much bow ties, Volvos, and horn-rimmed glasses, thank you very much.

My point is simple: This is a social decision, not a moral one or even an economic one. He has decided not to define himself in terms of a red Porsche convertible. He wants what his consumption community wants. But this opens up such an interesting question, at least to me. Why have academics proved such myopic observers of the consumerist world? Why so universally dour and critical? And why can't they see that their own buying habits are more a matter of taste than degree?

I think one reason we academics have been so unappreciative of the material world, often so downright snotty about it, is that we don't need it. Academics say they don't need it because they have the life of the mind, they have art, they contemplate the best that has been thought and said. (Plus, not a whole lot of disposable income.)

But that's not the entire story. I think that another reason most academics don't need store-bought affiliation is that the school world, like the church world it mimics, is a cosseted world, a world in which rank and order are well known and trusted and stable. In fact, buying stuff is more likely to confuse status than illuminate it.

Let me tell you who I am in this context. I am a professor in the English department at the University of Florida; I teach Romanticism. Members of my cohort know what the title "professor" means; they know how English fits into the academic food chain; they know where Florida ranks as a university; and they know Romanticism is not as hot as theory nor as cool as race/class/gender. If you are an academic, I instantly know about you from just a few words. Just say something like "I am a visiting assistant professor of sociology at Podunk U.," and I can pretty accurately spin a description of what your life has been like. Give me a bit more, like a publication cite (not the subject, but where it appears), and you are flying right into my radar. This system of social place is so stable that you wear it like a pair of Gucci sunglasses or an old-school tie. Little wonder academics are so perplexed by an outside world that seems preoccupied with social place via consumption. Little wonder we misunderstand it. I can't imagine what it would be like to tell people I was a CFO of a pre-IPO dot-com. I'd much rather just have them check out my nifty chunky loafers from Prada and my Coach edition of Lexus out in the driveway.

Most of us, yes, even academics, are living in a time of intense extropersonal relationships (in Latin, extro means "outward"), in which the focus on things, on people as things, on relationships as things, defines modern meanings. Look at how we define relationships in economic terms: Is he or she worth the trouble? This relationship is costing me too much. Where's the payoff?

Cost-benefit analysis is second nature to our language because it is second nature to our perceptions, regardless of how far we are from the marketplace. However, we may be reaching the point where the center of such a system will not hold, things fall apart, and, like it or not, we find ourselves moving away from defining the self via goods, because positional goods have become too plentiful and thus not meaningful enough.

As so many luxuries become necessities, maybe the concept of luxury is being drained of meaning. As the standard of living has risen, erstwhile luxury is becoming the norm. Since the 1970s we have been defining luxury downward into ordinary goods and services, even as we have increased our ability to consume objects and sensations hitherto beyond our reach. Perhaps the social construction of luxury is unraveling. Maybe we are indeed slouching toward Utopia.

When I mentioned the possible disappearance of luxury as a distinction to a friend who is the creative director of a large Midwestern advertising agency, his eyes lit up. One of his clients is a manufacturer of specialty faucets. When the agency tested images of kitchens that women felt reflected their sense of comfort and ease, the deluxe kitchen, complete with all the yuppie appliances, tested surprisingly low. What was high? The old-fashioned Kenmore-type kitchen, in which the appliances looked like what they were instead of pieces of commercialized, built-in elegance. It was, he said, as if the women were tired of seeing themselves as perfectionists and yearned for the more relaxed life of their mothers or grandmothers. Restoration Hardware may really be on to something more than nostalgia.

Perhaps the mass class of consumers has been living in the lap of luxury for too long. We used to be on the outside looking in. Now millions of us are inside looking out. Who knows? Maybe the very ubiquity of luxury will cause us to recharge human relationships and deflate material values.

The question then becomes: Are we better off for living in a culture in which luxuries are turned into necessities, mild addictions are made into expected tastes, elegancies are made niceties, expectancies are made entitlements, opulence is made into populence?

The answer, from the point of view of those historically excluded, is yes. Absolutely, yes. Ironically, just as the very stuff that I often find unaesthetic and others may find contemptible has ameliorated the condition of life for many, many millions of people, the very act of getting to this stuff promises a better life for others. I don't mean to belittle the value of religion, politics, law, education, and all the other patterns of meaning making in the modern world, but only to state the obvious. Forget happiness; if decreasing pain and discomfort is a goal, consumption of the "finer things" has indeed done what governments, churches, schools, and even laws have promised. Far more than these other systems, betterment through consumption has delivered the goods. Paul Krugman is certainly correct when he writes, "On sheer material grounds one would almost surely prefer to be poor today than upper middle class a century ago."

But is it fair? Do some of us suffer inordinately for the excesses of others? What are we going to do when all this stuff we have shopped for becomes junk? What about the environment? How close is the connection between the accumulation of the new luxury and the fact that the United States leads the industrialized world in rates of murder, violent crime, juvenile violent crime, imprisonment, divorce, abortion, single-parent households, obesity, teen suicide, cocaine consumption, per-capita consumption of all drugs, pornography production, and pornography consumption? What are we going to do about the lower sixth of our population that seems mired in transgenerational poverty?

These are important questions but ones I will leave to others. Entire academic, governmental, and commercial industries are dedicated to each of them. One of the more redemptive aspects of cultures that produce the concept of luxury is that they also produce the real luxury of having time and energy to discuss it. Who knows? Perhaps the luxury of reflection will help resolve at least some of the shortcomings of consumption.

Romanticism, my putative field of study, still informs much of the academic interpretation of commercialism. I am often reminded of something my mother told me. Her father ran a country store in the small town of Shelburne, Vt. During the Depression he sold on credit. And how did he know to whom to extend credit? He did it by smell, aroma profiling. Smell of horses, good; cows not so good, pigs and sheep bad. Shelburne is such a pretty little town: church, library, town hall, and community green. After the war, she and her siblings couldn't wait to get the hell out of there.

Let's face it: The idea that consumerism creates artificial desires rests on a wistful ignorance of history and human nature, on the hazy, romantic feeling that there existed some halcyon era of noble savages with purely natural needs. Once fed and sheltered, our needs have always been cultural, not natural. Until there is some other system to codify and satisfy those needs and yearnings, capitalism—and the promise of the better life it carries—will continue not just to thrive but to triumph, Muslim extremists and periodic recessions notwithstanding.

While you don't have to like needless consumption, let alone participate in it, it doesn't hurt to understand it and our part in it. We have not been led astray by marketers of unnecessary goods. It would be nice to think that this eternally encouraging market for top-of-the-line products will result in the cosmopolitanism envisioned by the Enlightenment philosophies, that a universalism of the new luxury will end in a crescendo of hosannas. It would be nice to think that more and more of the poor and disenfranchised will find their ways into the cycle of increased affluence without contracting the dreaded affluenza or, worse, luxury fever. It would be nice to think that commercialism could be heroic, self-abnegating, and redemptive. It would be nice to think that greater material comforts—more and more luxuries—will release us from racism, sexism, terrorism, and ethnocentrism and that the apocalypse will come as it did at the end of Romanticism, in Shelley's Prometheus Unbound, leaving us, "Sceptreless, free, uncircumscribed ... Equal, unclassed, tribeless, and nationless ... Pinnacled dim in the intense inane."

But the globalization of the new luxury is more likely to result in the banalities of an ever-increasing, worldwide consumerist culture. Recall that Athens ceased to be a major power around 400 BC, yet for centuries afterward Greek culture was the culture of the Mediterranean world. The age of European expansion ended in the mid-20th century; the age of luxury markets may be losing steam in North America, but it is just starting to gather force elsewhere. Academic Marxists love to refer to this as late capitalism. Early capitalism is probably more like it.

We have been in this lap of luxury a short time, and it is an often scary and melancholy place. This is a world not driven by the caprices of the rich, as was the first Gilded Age. Nor is it being whipsawed by marketers eager to sell crapulous products. They contribute, to be sure. But our world is being driven primarily by the often crafty and seemingly irrational desires of the mass class of consumers, most of them young. In many ways this is more frightening. A butterfly flapping its wings in China may not cause storm clouds over Miami, but a few lines of computer code written by some kid on his Palm Pilot in Palo Alto or Calcutta may indeed change life for all the inhabitants of Prague. Worse still, a Fendi purse or a Lexus automobile or a weekend at the Bellagio may be better understood by more people than the plight of the homeless, a Keats ode, or the desecration of the rain forest. Whatever it becomes, the mass-mediated and mass-marketed world of the increasingly powerful information age is drawing us ever closer together. The act of wanting what we don't need is indeed doing the work of a generation of idealists. Terrorism is a perverse tribute to its power.

We have not been led into this world of material closeness and shared desires against our better judgment. For many of us, especially when young, consumerism is our better judgment. Getting to luxury is a goal. And this is true regardless of class or culture. We have not just asked to go this way; we have demanded. Now most of the world is lining up, pushing and shoving, eager to elbow into the mall to buy what no one needs. Woe to the government or religion that says no. They don't seem to last for long.

As I have argued elsewhere, getting and spending have been the most passionate, and often the most imaginative, endeavors of modern life. We have done more than acknowledge that the good life starts with the material life, as the ancients did. We have made consuming stuff, most of it unnecessary stuff, the dominant prerequisite of organized society. Consumption has become production, especially at the high end in the category of luxury. That we should be unified by sharing this material and the stories that brands tell is dreary and depressing to some, as doubtless it should be. Remember Oscar Wilde's observation that "the brotherhood of man is no mere poet's dream, it is a most depressing and humiliating reality"? But one should not forget that the often vulgar, sensational, immediate, trashy, tribalizing, wasteful, equitable, sometimes transcendent, and unifying force of consuming the unnecessary is liberating and democratic to many more.

Reading Number 3: The Dubious Rewards of Consumption
by Alan Thein Durning (*New Renaissance magazine Vol.3, No.3*)

The avarice of mankind is insatiable," wrote Aristotle 23 centuries ago, describing the way that as each desire is satisfied, a new one seems to appear in its place. That observation forms the first precept of economic theory, and is confirmed by much of human experience. A century before Christ, the Roman philosopher Lucretius wrote: "We have lost our taste for acorns. So (too) we have abandoned those couches littered with herbage and heaped with leaves. So the wearing of wild beasts' skins has gone out or fashion....Skins yesterday, purple and gold today--such are the baubles that embitter human life with resentment."

Nearly 2,000 years later, Leo Tolstoy echoed Lucretius: "seek among men, from beggar to millionaire, one who is contented with his lot, and you will not find one such in a thousand....Today we must buy an overcoat and galoshes, tomorrow, a watch and a chain; the next day we must install ourselves in an apartment with a sofa and a bronze lamp; then we must have carpets and velvet gowns; then a house, horses and carriages, paintings and decorations."

Contemporary chroniclers of wealth concur. For decades Lewis Lapham, born into an oil fortune, has been asking people how much money they would need to be happy. "No matter what their income," he reports, "a depressing number of Americans believe that if only they had twice as much, they would inherit the estate of happiness promised them in the Declaration of Independence. The man who receives $15,000 a year is sure that he could relieve his sorrow if he had only $30,000 a year; the man with $1 million a year knows that all would be well if he had $2 million a year....Nobody," he concludes, "ever has enough."

If human desires are in fact infinitely expandable, consumption is ultimately incapable of providing fulfillment--a logical consequence ignored by economic theory. Indeed, social scientists have found striking evidence that high-consumption societies, just as high-living individuals, consume ever more without achieving satisfaction. The allure of the consumer society is powerful, even irresistible, but it is shallow nonetheless.

Measured in constant dollars, the world's people have consumed as many goods and services since 1950 as all previous generations put together. Since 1940, Americans alone have used up as large a share of the earth's mineral resources as did everyone before them combined Yet this historical epoch of titanic consumption appears to have failed to make the consumer class any happier. Regular surveys by the National Opinion Research Centre of the University of Chicago reveal, for example, that no more Americans report they are "very happy" now than in 1957. The "very happy" share of the population has fluctuated around one-third since the mid-fifties, despite near-doubling in both gross national product and personal consumption expenditures per capita.

A landmark study in 1974 revealed that Nigerians, Filipinos, Panamanians, Yugoslavians, Japanese, Israelis, and West Germans all ranked themselves near the middle on a happiness scale. Confounding any attempt to correlate material prosperity with happiness, low-income Cubans and affluent Americans both reported themselves considerably happier than the norm, and citizens of India and the Dominican Republic, less so. As psychologist Michael Argyle writes, "There is very little difference in the levels of reported happiness found in rich and very poor countries."

Any relationship that does exist between income and happiness is relative rather than absolute. The happiness that people derive from consumption is based on whether they consume more than their neighbors and more than they did in the past. Thus, psychological data from diverse societies such as the United States, the United Kingdom, Israel, Brazil, and India show that the top income strata tend to be slightly happier than the middle strata, and the bottom group tends to be the least happy. The Upper classes in any society are more satisfied with their lives than the lower classes are, but they are no more satisfied than the upper classes of much poorer countries--nor than the upper classes were in the less affluent past. Consumption is thus a treadmill, with everyone judging their status by who is ahead and who is behind.

That treadmill yields some absurd results. During the casino years of the mid-eighties, for example, many New York investment bankers who earned "only" $600,000 a year felt poor, suffering anxiety and self-doubt. On less than $600,000, they simply were unable to keep up with the Joneses. One despondent dealmaker lamented, "I'm nothing. You understand that, nothing. I earn $250,000 a year, but it's nothing, and I'm nobody."

From afar, such sentiments appear to reflect unadulterated greed. But on closer inspection they look more like evidence of humans' social nature. We are beings who need to belong. In the consumer society, that need to be valued and respected by others is acted out through consumption. As one Wall Street banker put it to the New York Times, "Net worth equals self-worth." Buying things becomes both a proof of self-esteem ("I' m worth it," chants one shampoo advertisement) and a means to social acceptance--a token of what turn-of-the-century economist Thorstein Veblen termed "pecuniary decency." Much consumption is motivated by this desire for approval: wearing the right clothes, driving the right car, and living in the right quarters are all simply says of saying, "I'm OK. I'm in the group."

In much the same way that the satisfaction of consumption derives from matching or outdoing others, it also comes from outdoing last year. Thus individual happiness is more a function of rising consumption that of high consumption as such. The reason, argues Stanford University economist Tibor Scitovsky, is that consumption is addictive: each luxury quickly becomes a necessity, and a new luxury must be found. This is as true for the young Chinese factory worker exchanging a radio for a black-and-white television as it is for the Sherman junior executive trading in a BMW for a Mercedes.

Luxuries become necessities between generations as well. People measure their current material comforts against the benchmark set in their own childhood. So each generation needs more than the previous did to be satisfied. Over a few generations, this process can redefine prosperity as poverty. The ghettos of the United States and Europe have things such as televisions that would have awed the richest neighborhoods of centuries past, but that does not diminish the scorn the consumer class heaps on slum dwellers, nor the bitterness belt by the modernized poor. With consumption standards perpetually rising, society is literally insatiable. The definition of a "decent" standard of living--the necessities of life for a member in good standing in the consumer society-endlessly shifts upward. The child whose parents have not purchased the latest video game feels ashamed to invite friends home. Teenagers without an automobile do not feel equal to their peers. In the clipped formulation of economists, "Needs are socially defined, and escalate with the rate of economic progress."

The relationships between consumption and satisfaction are thus subtle, involving comparisons over time and with social norms. Yet studies on happiness indicate a far less subtle fact as well. The main determinants of happiness in life are not related to consumption at all--prominent among them are satisfaction with family life, especially marriage, followed by satisfaction with work, leisure to develop talents, and friendships.

These factors are all an order of magnitude more significant than income in determining happiness, with the ironic result that, for example, suddenly striking it rich can make people miserable. Million-dollar lottery winners commonly become isolated from their social networks, lose the structure and meaning that work Formerly gave their lives, and find themselves estranged from even close friends and family. Similarly, analysts such as Scitovsky believe that reported happiness is higher at higher incomes largely because the skilled jobs of the well-off are more interesting than the routine labor of the working class. Managers, directors, engineers, consultants, and the rest of the professional elite enjoy more challenging and creative pursuits, and therefore receive more psychological rewards, than those lower on the business hierarchy.

Oxford University psychologist Michael Argyle's comprehensive work The Psychology of Happiness concludes: "The conditions of life which really make a difference to happiness are those covered by three sources-social relations, work and leisure. And the establishment of a satisfying state of affairs in these sphere does not depend much on wealth, either absolute or relative." Indeed, some evidence suggests that social relations, especially in households and communities, are neglected in the consumer society; leisure likewise tares worse among the consumer class than many assume.

The consumer society fails to deliver on its promise of fulfillment through material comforts because human wants are insatiable, human needs are socially defined, and the real sources of personal happiness are elsewhere. Indeed, the strength of social relations and the quality of leisure--both crucial psychological determinants of happiness in life--appear as much diminished as enhanced in the consumer class. The consumer society, it seems, has impoverished us by raising our income.

Reading Set Number Two: The Laborer

Problem: If people were aware of the conditions under which the stuff they buy was produced, would they modify their consumption habits?

Exercise: Do a brief inventory of your clothes closet and bureau and note the countries in which your clothes were assembled. Assume that the labor costs of the item were 25% of the cost and that the worker who assembled the garment was paid about 20% of what a U.S. worker was paid. If you raised the cost of each item by, say, 50 percent, would you have still purchased it?

Labor is as central to the culture of capitalism as consumption. The money that people use to consume generally comes from the sale of their own labor. Laborers are required to manufacture the stuff that other laborers, as consumers, buy. But perhaps more importantly, the price of labor often dictates the price of commodities. Yet, for some reason, the price of labor is often hidden from us. That is, when we buy the latest video game, the stylish pair of running shoes, the cup of coffee or mother's day bouquet, we rarely think about the labor that went into producing the product. Consequently we are often unaware of the labor conditions under which our purchases are produced. But should we be and, if we were, would it alter our patterns of consumption? The following two articles address labor conditions; the first examines the use of prison labor in production, the second looks at the conditions under which workers in the flower trade work.

The arguments regarding the use of low-paid workers are complex. On the one hand, some argue that the wages are well below what are required to lift people out of poverty; others argue, on the other hand, that the industries paying low wages are providing jobs that would otherwise be unavailable. See what you think.

Study Questions 2

1. What are some of the arguments against private business using prison labor?

2. What are some of the arguments that private business and prison authorities use regarding the propriety of business using prison labor?

3.What are some of the dangers that workers face on Ecuadorian flower farms?

4. What are some of the difficulties instituting and enforcing safe working conditions in Third World industries such as Ecuadorian flower farms?

Reading Number 1: Slave labor means big bucks for U.S. corporations By Michael Schwartz (Daily Bruin U. California-Los Angeles January 31, 2001)

(U-WIRE) LOS ANGELES—It seemed like a normal factory closing. U.S. Technologies sold its electronics plant in Austin, Texas, leaving its 150 workers unemployed. Everyone figured they were moving the plant to Mexico, where they would employ workers at half the cost. But six weeks later, the electronics plant reopened in Austin in a nearby prison.

At the same time, the United States blasts China for the use of prison slave labor, engaging in the same practice itself. Prison labor is a pot of gold. No strikes, union organizing, health benefits, unemployment insurance or workers' compensation to pay. As if exploiting the labor of prison inmates was not bad enough, it is legal in the United States to use slave labor. The 13th Amendment of the Constitution states that "neither slavery nor involuntary servitude, except as a punishment for crime whereof the party shall have been duly convicted shall exist within the United States."

There are approximately 2 million people behind bars in the United States—more than three times the number of prisoners in 1980. The United States now imprisons more people than any other country in the world. In fact, in the last 20 years California has constructed 21 new prisons while in the same amount of time, it has built only one new university. That statistic is even more astounding when we think about the fact that it took California almost 150 years to build its first 12 prisons. Another five new prisons are under construction and plans are in the works to build another 10.

The question that needs to be answered is—why? Why are prisons such a booming business? The answer lies in the prison industrial complex. At the same time that prisons clear the streets of those you feel are a "threat" to society, prisons also offer jobs in construction, guarding, administration, health, education and food service.

Prisons in impoverished areas often end up with inmates from the local area who had previously worked in the community. Often they were laid off from a factory job that moved overseas and they turned to alcohol or drugs, which ultimately landed them in prison. Others are luckier and get a job in the prison. One of the fastest-growing sectors of the prison industrial complex is private corrections companies. Private prisons also have an incentive to gain as many prisoners as possible and to keep them there as long as possible.

Many corporations, whose products we consume on a daily basis, have learned that prison labor can be as profitable as using sweatshop labor in developing nations. You might have had a first-hand experience with a prison laborer if you have ever booked a flight on Trans World Airlines, since many of the workers making the phone reservations are prisoners. Other companies that use prison labor are Chevron, IBM, Motorola, Compaq, Texas Instruments, Honeywell,

Microsoft, Victoria's Secret and Boeing. Federal prisons operate under the trade name Unicor and use their prisoners to make everything from lawn furniture to congressional desks. Their Web site proudly displays "where the government shops first."

Federal safety and health standards do not protect prison labor, nor do the National Labor Relations Board policies. The corporations do not even have to pay minimum wage. In California, inmates who work for the Prison Industrial Authority earn wages between 30 and 95 cents per hour before required deductions for restitutions and fines.

State Corrections agencies are even advertising their prisoners to corporations by asking these questions: "Are you experiencing high employee turnover? Worried about the cost of employee benefits? Getting hit by overseas competition? Having trouble motivating your work force? Thinking about expansion space? Then the Washington State Department of Corrections Private Sector Partnerships is for you."

Prisons are being filled largely with the poor, the mentally ill, people of color, drug addicts and many combinations of these characteristics. They are not reserved for violent people who are extremely dangerous to society.

In fact, of the nearly 2 million prisoners, about 150,000 are armed robbers, 125,000 are murderers and 100,000 are sex offenders. Prisons are certainly not filled with corporate criminals who make up only 1 percent of our nation's prisons.

In California, then-Gov. Pete Wilson signed the "three strikes and you're out" law in 1994. The law states that if an offender has two or more previous serious or violent felony convictions, the mandatory sentence for any new felony conviction is 25 years to life. Though people thought the three-strikes law was intended to protect society from dangerous career criminals, the actual enactment of the law has been dramatically different.

Kendall Cooke was convicted under the three-strikes law for stealing one can of beer with two previous convictions of theft. Clarence Malbrough was sentenced to 25 years to life for stealing batteries, a crime that would usually send someone to jail for about 30 days. Eddie Jordan stole a shirt from a JC Penney store, Juan Murro attempted to steal wooden pallets from a parking lot and Michael Garcia stole a package of steaks from a grocery store. All of these people are facing life in prison for petty theft. They are fueling the prison industry. They are not the exception, either.

Eighty-five percent of those sentenced under the law in California faced prison for a nonviolent offense. Two years after the law went into effect, there were twice as many people imprisoned under the three-strikes law for possession of marijuana as for murder, rape and kidnapping combined. More than 80 percent of those sentenced under the three-strikes law are African-American and Latino.

In the 1980s, Congress established several different mandatory minimum sentences. These laws require offenders of certain crimes to receive fixed sentences without parole. Mandatory sentences, especially for drugs, are largely responsible for the ever-increasing number of people behind bars in the United

States. In May of 1998, drug defendants made up 60 percent of the federal prison population, up from 25 percent in 1980. The disproportionate number of African Americans being sent to prison for drug use, however, is largely due to racism in the actual mandatory minimum laws themselves.

Though crack and powdered cocaine are virtually the same drug (crack is powder cocaine mixed with baking soda) possession of five grams of crack gets you a mandatory five years in jail, while it takes 500 grams of powdered cocaine to get this same sentence. The U.S. Sentencing Commission reported that in 1995, whites accounted for 52 percent of all crack users and African Americans, 38 percent. But just 4.1 percent of those sentenced for crack offenses are white, while 88 percent are African Americans. Seventy percent of our nation's prisons are made up of African Americans.

You now know that they are there through a variety of unjust racist laws.

Corporations are happily using these people for slave labor, which is perfectly legal under the constitution. Almost 2 million human beings are now locked up in our nation's prisons. The vast majority are not there because they are murderers, rapists or other violent people. They are there because prisons are a business in this country, whether we're talking about private prisons or private companies using prison labor. The next time you think of prison slave labor you don't have to think of China, think of the United States. And go take a look at the 13th Amendment.

CAYAMBE, Ecuador, Feb. 10 — In just five years, Ecuadorean roses, as big and red as the human heart, have become the new status flower in the United States, thanks to the volcanic soil, perfect temperatures and abundant sunlight that help generate $240 million a year and tens of thousands of jobs in this once-impoverished region north of Quito.

This St. Valentine's Day, hundreds of American florists and catalogs are offering the roses of this fertile valley. Calyx & Corolla, for instance, bills it as a place "where Andean mists and equatorial sun conspire to produce roses that quickly burst into extravagant bloom, then hold their glory long after lesser specimens have begun to droop."

But roses come with thorns, too. As Ecuador's colorful blooms radiate romance around the world, large growers here have been accused of misusing a toxic mixture of pesticides, fungicides and fumigants to grow and export unblemished pest-free flowers.

As in other industries like garment production, bananas and diamonds, the poor worry about eating first and labor conditions later. They toil here despite headaches and rashes here for the wealthier of the world, who in turn know little of the conditions in which their desires are met.

Doctors and scientists who have worked here say serious health problems have resulted for many of the industry's 50,000 workers, more than 70 percent of them women. Researchers say their work is hampered by lack of access to flower farms because of reluctant growers. But studies that the International Labor Organization published in 1999 and the Catholic University issued here last year showed that women in the industry had more miscarriages than average and that more than 60 percent of all workers suffered headaches, nausea, blurred vision or fatigue.

"No one can speak with conclusive facts in hand about the impact of this industry on the health of the workers, because we have not been able to do the necessary studies," said Dr. Bolívar Vera, a health specialist at the Health Environment and Development Foundation in Quito. "So the companies have been able to wash their hands of the matter."

In the 20 years since the farms started here, Ecuador has out of nowhere become the fourth-largest producer of roses in the world, with customers from Kazakhstan to Kansas.

St. Valentine's Day is the biggest rose event in the United States, which buys more than 70 percent of its cut flowers from South America and is Ecuador's biggest trading partner. Roses retail for up to $6 a bloom. Last week, workers at

RosaPrima, a plantation here, moved at a dizzying pace to cut, wrap and box 70,000 stems a day. Computers help supervisors track each stem and each worker's productivity.

The general manager, Ross Johnson, said he was proud of his business and especially his workers. He said that a doctor visited the farm several times a week and that all workers wore gloves and protective equipment, whether or not handling chemicals. Mr. Johnson said he had cracked down on contractors who hired children as temporary workers.

"We have made a lot of improvements over the years," said Mr. Johnson, who was born in Ecuador and who helped start the farm seven years ago. "I think this is a noble business that does noble things for people here and around the world."

He said roses were typically fumigated 24 hours before being cut. Then they are soaked overnight in a nontoxic chemical solution and shipped at near freezing temperatures.

Dr. César Paz-y-Miño, a geneticist at the Catholic University, said several pesticides used on a farm that was the setting for his research in the late 1990's were restricted as health hazards in other countries, including the United States, and labeled as highly toxic by the World Health Organization.

Among the most notorious are captan, aldicarb and fenamiphos. Dr. Paz-y-Miño refused to identify the flower farm under an agreement that he said he had with the owners.

He described the conditions as astonishing and recalled workers' fumigating in street clothes without protective equipment, pesticides stored in poorly sealed containers and fumes wafting over the workers' dining halls. When asked what government agencies monitor worker health and safety, Dr. Paz-y-Miño said, "There are no such checks."

Neither the Labor nor Health Ministries have occupational health departments. In an interview, Labor Minister Felipe Mantilla said he planned to visit flower and banana plantations in a few weeks. Human rights groups, including Human Rights Watch, have criticized Ecuadorean banana growers for using child labor. Mr. Mantilla said the government planned to set up "discussion tables" for workers and managers to discuss competitiveness and labor conditions.

"If there are violations," he said, "we will act firmly. We are drawing up a plan of action on the issue of workers' conditions and we are seeking help from international organizations. The ministry does not have funds to implement plans for progressive control. So that is why we look for international help."

Industry representatives denied that there was a health problem or that unacceptable risks were taken.

"The growers we know are very conscious of environmental issues," said Harrison Kennicott, the chief executive of Kennicott Brothers, a wholesaler in Chicago who is a former president of the Society of American Florists, a trade group.

"They go to lengths to get certified environmentally," Mr. Kennicott said. "The growers take care of the people. They provide housing and medical care.

"Our job is to satisfy our customers, who are the florists and retailers who deliver flowers to the public. Our interest is having the best quality product at a competitive price."

Yet it is hard to erase images of workers like Soledad, 32, and Petrona, 34, both mothers and both looking jaundiced and bony. In interviews after quitting time, they asked not to be fully identified out of fear that they would lose their $156-a-month jobs cutting flowers in greenhouses. The women said they had elementary school educations but did not need high-level science to tell them why their kidneys throbbed at night and heads throbbed in the day.

"There is no respect for the fumigation rules," said Petrona, who has worked on flower farms for four years. "They spray the chemicals even while we are working."

"My hair has begun to fall out," she added, running a hand from the top of her visibly receding hairline down a single scruffy braid. "I am young, but I feel very old."

Soledad, who has worked on flower farms for 12 years, slowly turned her head from side to side.

"If I move my head any faster, I feel nauseous," she said, and then pulled up her sleeve to show her skeletal limbs. "I have no appetite."

When asked whether the farm where they worked had a doctor on duty, the women rolled their eyes.

"He always tells us there is nothing wrong with us and sends us back to work," Petrona said. "He works for the company. He does not help us."

The industry received a helping hand from the Andean Trade Preference Act of 1991. It gives tariff-free access to American markets for farmers in Bolivia, Colombia, Ecuador and Peru. The law was intended as part of Washington's fight against drug trafficking, offering incentives to abandon coca and poppy growing.

Roses have become one of the top five sources of export revenue for Ecuador. The bloom boom has transformed this once sleepy region of cattle ranches, inhabited primarily by Indians. Much of the heartland has been hollowed out by illegal immigration to Europe and the United States, but the population in the flower regions north and south of Quito has soared. In Cayambe, the population has increased in 10 years, from 5,000 to more than 70,000.

Flowers have helped pave roads and built sophisticated irrigation systems. This year, construction will begin on an international airport between Quito and Cayambe.

The average flower worker earns more than the $120-a-month minimum wage. By employing women, the industry has fostered a social revolution in which mothers and wives have more control over their families' spending, especially on schooling for their children.

As it has grown successful, the industry has come under fire from the green movement in Europe and was the subject of a recent article in Mother Jones magazine. European consumers have pressed for improvements and environmental safeguards, encouraging some growers to join a voluntary program aimed at helping customers identify responsible growers. The certification signifies that dozens of the 460 growers have distributed protective gear, given training in using chemicals and hired doctors to visit at least weekly.

"There are still farms that do not respect fumigation limits or give workers proper training and equipment for handling chemicals," said Gonzalo Luzuriaga, chief executive officer of BellaRosa, another flower grower here. "But many of the farmers are very conscientious about these issues, and we are working to make improvements."

Still numerous signs remain that life for the workers, although better, is far from good. Looking over the town plaza from his second-floor office, Mayor Diego Bonifaz, who also operates a flower farm, said: "It's hard for me to get the wealth out of the plantations and into the community. The farms operate in the first world, selling flowers on the Internet. I am still struggling to pave streets."

Reliable health care, however, seems the most glaring need. Beds have been added to the local hospital, doctors said, but workers often cannot afford services there. The chief of the Red Cross clinic, Dr. Toribio Valladares, said he had seen growing numbers of people with respiratory problems, conjunctivitis, miscarriages and rashes, although he did not have firm numbers.

Like the two women who harvest greenhouse roses, Dr. Valladares voiced deep distrust of doctors who worked on the flower farms.

"When the workers go for help to the doctors on the plantations," he said, "the doctors treat the symptoms but do not examine the workers to try to determine their illnesses. And the doctors always tell them that their illnesses have nothing to do with their work."

In Miami, James Pagano, chief marketing officer of Calyx & Corolla, said he had not been to Ecuador and did not want to comment on environmental or worker conditions.

"We buy what we think consumers will perceive to be a high quality rose at a competitive price," he said. The environment "is not an issue we have any business being in."

Reading Set Number Three: The Capitalist

Problem: Why has free-market capitalism failed to deliver on its promise of bringing poverty reduction and increased economic equality to peripheral countries?

Exercise: Some argue that for global wealth to be equally distributed, everyone would need to adopt a standard of living that people in the rich nations of the world would define as poverty. How much of your standard of living would you be willing to give up to contribute to the equitable global distribution of wealth?

In 1949, President Harry Truman addressed congress and, for the first time, used the term "economic development." The world, so people assumed, was divided into two areas: the developed consisting largely of the industrialized nations of Europe, North America and Asia, and the undeveloped non-industrial nations largely of South and Central America and Africa. This division could have been phrased in other ways (e.g. colonial and colonized nations), but the goal was to bring the perceived benefits and standard of living from industrial to non-industrial nations. There were, of course, many hidden assumptions in the term "economic development," not the least of which was that one set of nations that promoted trade and economic development was advanced, while the others, less reliant on trade and growth, were "backward." It is these assumptions that have driven what is referred to today as "globalization," the spread of the free market economy from one part of the world to the other. Free market capitalism was supposed to raise everyone's standard of living. The problem is that it hasn't quite worked out as planned, and billions of the world's people live in poverty without the money necessary in a free-market, capitalist economy, to purchase the basic necessities of life--food, shelter, basic health care, and education. The problem is why hasn't free-market capitalism delivered on its promise and why, in fact, do billions find themselves worse off than before 1949?

The first paper in this set of Talking Points readings, The Unremarkable Record of Liberalized Trade reports that efforts to promote "free trade" have failed. Multilateral institutions created to promote economic development and free trade have failed to help the vast majority of the world's poor, in spite of promises to the contrary. These institutions, such as the World Bank, the International Monetary Fund (IMF) and World Trade Organizations (WTO) have, the authors argue, increased poverty and economic inequality. For example, in spite of increased unregulated capital flows (money moving from one country to another) to developing countries, poverty and inequality has increased.

But if free-market capitalism has failed to reduce poverty and economic inequality, what are the other alternatives?

31

In the second article of the set David J. Rothkopf warns that, particularly in America, people may be overconfident of economic dominance and growth, and that the failure of free-market capitalism to ease poverty, will promote revolutionary responses. By failing to directly address these problems, says Rothkopf, we create the conditions for resistance. Rothkopf believes, however, that capitalism, if it succeeds in giving more people a stake in the economy, can address these problems.

The third article by David Korten examines the nature and consequences of money and investment and questions whether or not our definition of "wealth" itself, and our notion of acceptable "standard of living," needs reexamination.

Study Questions 3

1. Why, according to the authors, does an increase in unregulated capital (money) mobility and trade liberalization tend to increase poverty and economic inequality?

2. For what reasons do the authors believe that the World Bank underestimates the extent of poverty and economic inequality?

3. What is the warning that David J. Rothkopf issues in his article?

4. What solution does Rothkopf offer to allow capitalism to live up to its promise of reducing poverty and promoting economic equality?

5. According to Korten what is the difference between a real market economy on the one hand and global capitalism on the other?

6. How did the Asian financial crisis of 1997 reveal the flaws in global capitalism?

Reading Number 1: The unremarkable record of liberalized trade by Christian E. Weller, Robert E. Scott and Adam S. Hersh. (Economic Policy Institute Briefing Papers, Oct 2001)

Recently, a growing number of policy makers have touted the potential for global economic integration to combat poverty and economic inequity in the world today. On September 24, 2001, for instance, U.S. Trade Representative Robert Zoellick (2001), arguing for new "fast track" trade promotion authority, cited a World Bank study claiming that globalization "reduces poverty because integrated economies tend to grow faster and this growth is usually widely diffused". Yet the empirical evidence suggests that reductions in poverty and income inequality remain elusive in most parts of the world, and, moreover, that greater integration of deregulated trade and capital flows over the last two decades has likely undermined efforts to raise living standards for the world's poor.

In 1980, median income in the richest 10% of countries was 77 times greater than in the poorest 10%; by 1999, that gap had grown to 122 times. Inequality has also increased within many countries. Over the same period, any gains in poverty reduction have been relatively small and geographically isolated. The number of poor people rose from 1987 to 1998, and the share of poor people increased in many countries—in 1998 close to half the population were considered poor in many parts of the world. In 1980, the world's poorest 10%, or 400 million people, lived on 72 cents a day or less. The same number of people had 79 cents (nominally) per day in 1990 and 78 cents in 1999.

While many social, political, and economic factors contribute to poverty, the evidence shows that unregulated capital and trade flows contribute to rising inequality and impede progress in poverty reduction. Trade liberalization leads to more import competition and to a growing use of the threat to move production to lower-wage locales, thereby depressing wages. Deregulated international capital flows have led to rapid increases in short-term capital flows and more frequent economic crises, while simultaneously limiting the ability of governments to cope with crises. Economic upheavals disproportionately harm the poor, and thus contribute to the lack of success in poverty reduction and to rising income inequality.

The world's poor may stand to gain from global integration, but not under the unregulated version currently promoted by the World Bank and others. The lesson of the past 20 years is clear: it is time for a different approach to global integration, whereby living standards of the world's poor are raised rather than jeopardized.

Deregulated global trade and capital markets as the culprit

Over the past decades international capital mobility has grown as capital controls were reduced or eliminated virtually everywhere. Consequently, capital flows to developing countries have grown rapidly, from $1.9 billion in 1980 to $120.3 billion in 1997, the last year before the global financial crisis, or by more than 6,000%. Even in 1998, in the wake of the financial crisis, capital flows remained remarkably high at $56 billion. A substantial share of these capital flows (e.g., 36% in 1997) consisted of short-term portfolio investments.

Faster capital mobility in a relatively deregulated environment leads to rising inequality, both within countries and between countries, and to less poverty reduction or even increasing poverty.

The probability of financial crises in developing countries rises in direct relation to increases in unregulated short-term capital flows. Rising short-term capital inflows result in increased speculative financing and, subsequently, rising financial instability. Financial crises reduce the likelihood for the poor to escape poverty through economic growth because they are ill-equipped to weather the adverse macro-economic shocks. Financial crises also lower short-term growth rates, and it is estimated that poverty increases by 2% for every percent decline in growth.

The burdens of financial crisis are disproportionately borne by a country's poor. Since higher-income earners have better access to insurance mechanisms that protect them from the fallout of a crisis (including capital flight), macro-economic crises lead to a more unequal income distribution within countries. Thus, economic crises increase the need for well-functioning social safety nets. Yet unfettered capital flows limit governments' abilities to design policies to help the poor when they need it most—in the middle of a crisis. The International Monetary Fund often opposes increased government expenditures to assist the poor during economic crises, and investors withdraw their funds following increased government expenditures.

Finally, developing countries are prone to experience more severe economic crises with greater frequency than are developed economies, leading to greater inequality between countries.

Trade liberalization—the complement to deregulated capital markets in the global deregulation agenda—also plays a significant role in raising inequality and limiting efforts at poverty reduction. By inducing rapid structural change and shifting employment within industrializing countries, trade liberalization leads to falling real wages and declining working conditions and living standards.

Trade liberalization also gives teeth to employers' threats to close plants or to relocate or outsource production abroad—where labor regulations are less stringent and more difficult to enforce—and undermines workers' attempts to organize and bargain for improved wages and working conditions. This trend fuels a race to the bottom in which national governments vie for needed investment by bidding down the cost to employers (and livings standards) of working people.

The connection between rapid trade liberalization and inequality appears to be universal, indicating downward wage pressures and rising inequality following trade liberalization in industrializing and industrialized economies. A report by UNCTAD found that trade liberalization in Latin America led to widening wage gaps, falling real wages for unskilled workers (often more than 90% of the labor force in developing countries), and rising unemployment.

Rising inequality is common within many countries
Defenders of the current regime of global deregulation, including the World Bank, acknowledge that inequality has increased within countries. But in its most recent and rather comprehensive document on globalization and poverty (World Bank 2001a), the Bank raised two issues that supposedly mute the fact of rising intra-country inequality. First, data for China dwarfs observations for all other countries, thereby suggesting that rising inequality in globalizing countries does not exist outside of China. However, data for other countries show that growing inequality is indeed a widespread trend. Second, the World Bank also claimed that rising inequality is not a result of increasing poverty, which thus makes it presumably less troubling. While this claim may hold true in China, it does not describe the trend in many other parts of the world.

There is a broad consensus that income inequality has risen in industrialized countries since 1980. The World Bank reports that there was a "serious…increase in within-country inequality in industrialized countries reversing the trend of [the period 1950-80]" .Similarly, Gottschalk and Smeeding found that "almost all industrial economies experienced some increase in wage inequality among prime-aged males" in the 1980s and early 1990s. Further, data from the Luxembourg Income Study show that, among 24 countries, 18 experienced increasing income inequality, five (Denmark, Luxembourg, the Netherlands, Spain, and Switzerland) experienced declining inequality, and one (France) saw no change.

Income inequality is also rising in industrializing countries. There was been an unambiguous rise in inequality in Latin America in the 1980s and 1990s. Other areas also saw inequality rise in the 1980s and 1990s. Deininger and Squire found rising inequality in East Asia, Eastern Europe, and Central Asia since 1981, and growing polarization in South Asia. Only sub-Saharan Africa shows a trend toward more income equality since the 1980s.

While a widening gap between the rich and the poor within countries is not universal, it appears to have occurred at least in the majority of countries, and is affecting the income of the majority of people around the globe, contrary to claims by the World Bank that rising inequality within countries has been rare.

Poverty remains a large and widespread problem
The World Bank tries to divert attention from rising inequality by emphasizing its analyses of poverty reduction. It argues that "the long [term] trends of rising global inequality and rising numbers of people in absolute poverty have been halted and perhaps even reversed" due to greater globalization. However, the purported success in poverty reduction is elusive: the number of poor people is on the rise, relative poverty shares remain high in many parts of the world, and poverty shares are rising in many regions.

In assessing global poverty trends, the World Bank relies on a study that highlights the World Bank's *Global Poverty Monitoring* database and provides an overview of poverty trends from 1987 to 1998. The authors themselves, though, conclude that "[i]n the aggregate, and for some large regions, all…measures suggest that the 1990s did not see much progress against consumption poverty in the developing world". Also, the IMF reports that "[p]rogress in raising real incomes and alleviating poverty has been disappointingly slow in many developing countries."

The assessment of poverty trends by the World Bank suffers from several problems. First, measuring poverty is a difficult undertaking that can easily lead to errors. Different measures of poverty exist. The World Bank's *Global Poverty Monitoring* database, for example, uses an international poverty line of $1.08 per day in 1993 dollars based on purchasing power parity (PPP) exchange rates. But absolute poverty lines such as this one ignore regional or country-by-country differences.

The evidence shows that the use of an international poverty line tends to understate the share of people living in poverty, compared to other poverty measures. For example, a method using individual national poverty lines finds an additional 14% of the population to be considered poor compared to a method using the international poverty line. An alternative to both the national and international poverty line methods is to use a relative poverty line based on mean consumption or income levels in each country. Using such a relative poverty line instead of the international poverty line shows on average an additional 8% of the population to be considered poor.

Second, poverty lines are often inadequate to measure the true hardships people are facing in meeting the basic necessities of life. For instance, a recent U.S. study showed that 29% of working families did not earn enough to afford basic necessities, suggesting that a better approach to understanding poverty may lie in measuring household budgets rather than simple poverty lines.

The third problem with the Bank's poverty assessment is that even the poverty reduction gains it does find are small and geographically isolated. In 1998, the share of the population living in poverty in industrializing countries was 32%, under a relative poverty line. Although that percentage was down from 36% in 1987, the actual number of people living in poverty increased from 1.5 billion to 1.6 billion. In 1998, the share of the population in poverty remained very high in some regions: over 40% in South Asia and over 50% in sub-Saharan Africa and Latin America (**Table 1**). Since 1987, the share of the poor has stayed relatively constant in sub-Saharan Africa and Latin America but more than tripled in Eastern Europe and Central Asia.

TABLE 1					
Share of people living below relative poverty lines					
Geographic Area	1987	1990	1993	1996	1998
East Asia	33.01%	33.69%	29.82%	19.03%	19.56%
East Asia, excluding China	45.06	38.68	30.76	23.16	24.55
Eastern Europe and Central Asia	7.54	16.19	25.34	26.08	25.60
Latin America and Caribbean	50.20	51.48	51.08	51.95	51.35
Middle East and North Africa	18.93	14.49	13.62	11.40	10.76
South Asia	45.20	44.21	42.52	42.49	40.20
Sub-Saharan Africa	51.09	52.05	54.01	52.80	50.49
Share of world:					
Living under $1.08/day	28.31%	28.95%	28.15%	24.53%	23.96%
Living under relative poverty lines	36.31	37.41	36.73	32.79	32.08
Maximum daily consumption of world's poorest 400 million (nominal)	$0.79	$0.79	$0.56	$0.84	$0.75

Notes: The drop in 1993 reflects sharp decreases in per capita GDP in Nigeria, Ethiopia, Myanmar, and the Democratic Republic of Congo that, combined, made up 58% of the sample population in 1993.

Calculations for the world's poorest 400 million are based on average nominal per capita GDP.

Sources: Chen and Ravallion (2001); IMF (2001a, 2001b); and authors' calculations.

Another way to look at the global trends in poverty is to consider the incomes of an absolute number of poor people. Take, for instance, the poorest 10% of the population in 1980, consisting of about 400 million people, based on average per capita GDP. The poorest 400 million lived on a nominal $0.72 a day in 1980, $0.79 a day in 1990, $0.84 in 1996, and $0.78 in 1999 (Table 1). In other words, the income of the world's poorest did not even keep up with inflation. Clearly, the economic burden worsened for a large number of people in the 1990s.

Fourth, since the data do not extend beyond 1998, the full impact of the crises in Asia, Latin America, and Russia is not included, making it likely that future revisions will show less progress in poverty reduction. Lustig (2000) argues that frequent macroeconomic crises are the single most important cause of rapid increases in poverty in Latin America. Consequently, future revisions to the poverty trends in the late 1990s could show smaller average reductions or larger increases in the crisis-stricken areas. In fact, revisions to past data already show less success in poverty reduction than previously assumed. Chen and Ravallion, for example, show that the reduction of people living below the poverty line between 1987 and 1993 was not four percentage points, as estimated in 1997, but less than one percentage point.

Finally, the World Bank's conclusion that the lot of the poor has improved during the era of increasing trade and capital flow liberalization relies substantially on data from China and India, but the experiences of both countries are anomalies. In reality, the facts in these countries undermine the case for a connection between greater deregulation of capital and trade flows and falling poverty and inequality. While in China the percentage who are poor has fallen, there has been a rapid rise in inequality. Most notably, inequality between rural and urban areas and provinces with urban centers and those without grew from 1985 to 1995. Also, a large number of China's workers labor under abhorrent, and possibly worsening, slave or prison labor conditions. This situation not only means that many workers are left out of China's economic growth, it also makes China an unappealing development model for the rest of the world. Thus, improvements in China are not universally shared and leave many workers behind, often in deplorable conditions.

Using India to illustrate the benefits of unregulated globalization is equally problematic to the World Bank's position, since India's progress was accomplished while remaining relatively closed off to the global economy. Total goods trade (exports plus imports) was about 20% of India's gross domestic product in 1998, or 10 percentage points less than in China and only about one-fifth the level of such export-oriented countries as Korea. Moreover, that the IMF continuously recommended further liberalization of India's trade and capital flows—the only large developing economy for which this was the case—suggests that the IMF viewed India as a laggard in deregulating its economy.

Continued income divergence across countries (besides China)
The arguments on changes in income inequality between countries take a few perspectives. The World Bank's conclusion that incomes between countries are converging is based on differentiating between countries that have embraced unregulated globalization and those that have not. The World Bank's assertion

that "between countries, globalization is mostly reducing inequality" seems to contrast directly with the IMF's assessment that "the relative gap between the richest and the poorest countries has continued to widen" in the 1990s . Given this confusion, it is useful to take a global perspective that looks at all countries and the distribution of world income across all countries and across all people.

The distribution of world income between countries grew unambiguously in the 1980s and 1990s. In other words, rich countries have gotten richer and poor countries have gotten poorer (**Table 2**). The median per-capita income of the world's richest 10% of countries was 76.8 times that of the poorest 10% of countries in 1980, 119.6 times greater in 1990, and 121.8 times greater in 1999. The ratio of the average per capita incomes shows a similar, yet more dramatic, increase.

TABLE 2 Distribution of world income, ratio of top 10% to bottom 10%			
	1980	1990	1999
By countries			
Ratio of average incomes	86.2%	125.9%	148.8%
Ratio of median incomes	76.8	119.6	121.8
By population			
Ratio of average incomes	78.9	119.7	117.7
Ratio of median incomes	69.6	121.5	100.8
By population, excluding China			
Ratio of average incomes	90.3	135.5	154.4
Ratio of median incomes	81.1	131.2	153.2

Note: Distributions are based on per capita GDP in current U.S. dollars (IMF 2001a).

Source: Authors' calculations based on IMF (2001a, 2001b).

The distribution of world income across people, rather than countries, witnessed some equitable improvement in the 1990s after a dramatic increase in inequality during the 1980s. While the richest 10% of the world's population had, on average, incomes that were 78.9 times higher than those of the poorest 10% of the world population in 1980, their incomes were 119.7 times higher in 1990. That ratio dropped to 117.7 in 1999. The improvement in equality in the 1990s was somewhat more pronounced in terms of median incomes, yet even under this measure the distribution of incomes was remarkably more inequitable in 1999 than at the beginning of the period in 1980.

Furthermore, the gains in the 1990s come solely from rising incomes in China. If China is excluded, there is an unambiguous trend toward growing income inequality across the remaining world population in the 1980s and 1990s (Table 2). Without China, the richest 10% of the world population had, on average, 90.3 times as much income as the poorest 10% in 1980, 135.5 times more in 1990, and 154.4 times more in 1999. However, since China's income distribution has become substantially more unequal in the 1990s, including China's per capita GDP in the distribution of world income across all people exaggerates improvements in the world's income distribution in the 1990s. Thus, the world's income is significantly more unequally distributed at the end of the almost 20-year experiment with unregulated global capitalism than at the beginning of it.

Conclusion
Criticism of the unregulated globalization agenda has been met with policy makers' renewed adherence to the doctrine that greater global deregulation of trade and capital flows helps to improve inequality between countries, to raise equality within countries, and to accelerate poverty reduction. But income distribution between countries worsened in the 1980s, and its apparent improvement (or leveling off) in the 1990s is the result solely of rising per capita income in China, where the enormous population tends to distort world averages. Within-country income inequality is also growing and is a widespread trend in countries with both advanced and developing economies. Success in reducing poverty has been limited. The number of poor people has risen, and the share of poor people has grown in many areas, especially in Eastern Europe and Central Asia. And the share of poor people remained high at 40-50% in Latin America, sub-Saharan Africa, and South Asia.

The promises of more equal income distribution and reduced poverty around the globe have failed to materialize under the current form of unregulated globalization. Thus, it is time for multinational institutions and other international policy makers to develop a different set of strategies and programs to provide real benefits to the poor.

Reading Number 2: After This: Whatever Capitalism's Fate, Somebody's Already Working on an Alternative by David J. Rothkopf (Washington Post, January 19, 2002)

Somewhere in the world today walks the next Marx. But he is not a communist, and he almost certainly is not an expatriate German slaving over his theories in the stacks of the British Library. Nonetheless, he or she will attempt to seize upon the trends behind today's headlines to shape a competitor to "American capitalism" that the disenfranchised in nations around the world can embrace.

She may be in the streets of Buenos Aires, protesting an economic meltdown that has left her family in the dust. He may have been among the Palestinians celebrating at the collapse of the World Trade Center or among the Indonesians marching beneath banners bearing the likeness of Osama bin Laden. He may be in Beijing working to become the architect of reforms that might actually make "market socialism" a sustainable concept. She might be a Nigerian whose daughter is among the 25,000 children worldwide who die every day because, in the era of Perrier and artificial hearts, they lack clean water, basic medicine or food. He might even be a Russian seeking to reestablish that country's leadership with an approach that is an alternative to an increasingly self-interested, inflexible United States.

We may not know the region from which the next Marx will hail or his particular approach. But we can be sure that someone, somewhere will offer an alternative vision. And as America stands astride the world, the fact that so many of us, citizens of the most successful nation in history, think that such a threat to our values is impossible may be the very thing that will allow it to come true.

Never in the history of nations or ideas has there been an extended period in which one view has prevailed without challenge, particularly one that is seen by many to be widening the gaps between the world's comparatively few rich people and the great majority who are poor.

Rome was supposed to last forever, and fell. Kings ruled by divine right, and fell. The British Empire was the mightiest in the world but could not stand up against the will of its subjects. The Industrial Revolution was transformed when it generated a clamor for workers' rights and unions and communism itself. In business, what dominant brand has ever remained unchallenged? As Swiss watchmakers and American car makers, steel companies and television networks all know, the seeds of disaster lie in a triumph so great that it stifles the will to innovate, to evolve and to attend to the needs of the markets or peoples upon whom you depend for success.

The end of the Cold War was not, as some would have it, the End of History. It was, instead, the end of one challenge to capitalism. And if we do not recognize the costs of the hubristic interpretation of world affairs we have accepted during the past decade (that we are right and all others must play by our rules or founder), then we will be making it easier for a new generation of challenges to arise.

The harbingers of this looming threat are not just in the dissatisfaction of the world's poor. They also lie in the frustrations of America's allies at this moment of our undisputed greatness.

Recently, one of Latin America's senior diplomats—a known supporter of the United States—asked me, "What kind of message is America sending? In Argentina, they thought they were playing by U.S. rules, being a good friend to the United States, helping you from Haiti to Bosnia. And what was their reward? You turn away at their moment of greatest need. They are not alone in this feeling." He went on to say that many of America's friends in Latin America and elsewhere think that we are good at asking for cooperation, good at directing—and not so good at listening or giving.

This is not a new view. But recent events have exacerbated feelings of frustration with the United States on these points. A European politician with whom I spoke a few weeks ago complained about the so-called Bush Doctrine, the president's "Whose side are you on?" policy toward terrorism. This was not his idea of what an alliance should be. "It's a one-way street. You say we are either with your or against you. And who decides? America does." When I repeated this politician's reaction a few days later to a group of senior Asian military leaders, they laughed and nodded in agreement.

At the moment, the U.S. government talks a good game about engagement in the world, but the reality is in large part disengagement and self-absorption— just the sorts of approaches that leave openings and persuasive arguments for would-be rivals.

The war against terrorism is worthy, but it is really a war to protect Americans. From Latin America to Africa to Asia, any one of which may give rise to the next Marx, terrorists will wage their campaigns with little or no direct opposition from Washington. We talk of globalization but in the past eight years, since NAFTA and the Uruguay Round in 1994, Congress has primarily chosen a path of protection on trade issues and has made few major advances in the area of trade liberalization, with the exception of China's accession to the WTO. In the meantime, U.S. influence in international financial institutions has advanced policies that promote hard currencies and the interests of Wall Street above those of local populations to such an extent that they have triggered a backlash against the "Washington consensus"—a recipe for emerging markets reform that stresses privatization, market opening and trade liberalization. Indeed, to say "Washington institutions" in most of the world is to speak of rich man's rules.

Don't get me wrong. I'm no latter-day Che Guevara wandering out of the jungle. Quite the contrary. The radical reformer to whom I think we need to pay the most attention is none other than Margaret Thatcher. She championed the idea of a "nation of shareholders." When she became Britain's prime minister, 2 million people in her country owned stock. When she left office, there were seven times that. That shift transformed a nation that had viewed itself as consigned to stagnation and frustration into a world leader in innovation regardless of the political party at the helm.

This is where most of the reforms of the recent past have fallen short. This is where capitalism has let down most emerging markets. This is where the United States has created the greatest opportunity for anger and backlash. In the 1990s, the International Monetary Fund, banks and other advocates of the interests of advanced capitalist countries went around the world preaching the much-needed "Washington consensus" reforms. But they did not address the central issue bedeviling most emerging and less developed economies: ownership.

When governments sold their assets as part of privatization schemes, they were bought by those who had access to capital. These were either multinational corporations or powerful local business people with the assets and credit history to borrow to buy—in other words, the elites. When borders were opened or new capital flowed into the country, who benefited most? Those who already controlled the majority of local assets. Call them what you will: the chaebol of Korea, the former apparatchiks of Russia, the kleptocrats of Indonesia or the family-owned groups of Latin America, the elites and their closest associates in the international financial community benefited most from the reforms of the '90s.

But when troubled times led to austerity programs in these countries, it was the newly laid-off workers, small borrowers and others who were slammed when currencies were suddenly and artlessly devalued. Sure, plenty of big businesses faltered. But the benefits of reform were generally greater and problems far fewer for the elites. So, too, with globalization: Rich nations have benefited more than poor, while the number of those living in absolute poverty (or indeed starving) has risen starkly. According to Canadian Feed the Children, the richest 358 people in the world have a net worth equal to the combined annual income of the poorest 2.3 billion.

So, now again the cry of the populists is falling on receptive ears. That populism may take the form of the tragicomic economic policies of Eduardo Duhalde, Argentina's fifth head of state since mid-December, or the rhetoric of the increasingly paranoid and erratic Hugo Chavez in Venezuela. It may be the regionalism of Mahathir Mohamad in Malaysia or the nationalism of right-wing European or Japanese politicians. Or it may be a populism in which the alternative to American capitalism is not an economic theory, but is instead a reinterpreted religion like the twisted Islam of bin Laden.

The question is: Do we maintain the status quo and hope that the genuine magnificence of the American experience is persuasive to those for whom it is but a remote video image? Or do we recognize the challenges we face? Granted, the specter of communism no longer haunts us. Instead, there are only seeds growing in far-away fields, perverse seeds that thrive when neglected.

We must begin by recognizing that the genius of capitalism is not, as Treasury Secretary Paul O'Neill suggested recently, that it allows companies to die, but that it continually reinvents itself. Democracy shares this genius. We have made American capitalism work here and other brands of capitalism work elsewhere in the developed world. But we must recognize that we have not come close to perfecting global capitalism. We must create stakeholders in globalization, in capitalism and in democracy by reforming local systems so that the disenfranchised have access to the capital, education, legal institutions, market efficiencies and other benefits that can only come when the grasp of the elites on limited national assets is loosened and the opportunity to own and build wealth is genuinely offered. We must also focus on offering results soon, rather than succumbing to the maqana, maqana approach of the politically tone-deaf economists who authored many of today's problems.

The reason we didn't reach the End of History a few years back is that the global community failed to do as advertised. The issue that dogged us throughout the past 200 years and fostered the Cold War remained: How do you achieve the just distribution of wealth in society? That issue remains unanswered. But it is the nature of man to seek such answers. Experience teaches that either we recognize our responsibility to find them or we leave that to others who may attract great followings to dangerous and ill-considered ideas, just as Marx once did.

Reading Number 3: The Difference Between Money & Wealth by David Korten (*Business Ethics*, January/February 1999.

The capitalist economy has a potentially fatal ignorance of two subjects. One is the nature of money. The other is the nature of life. This ignorance leads us to trade away life for money, which is a bad bargain indeed.

The real nature of money is obscured by the vocabulary of finance, which is doublespeak. We use the term "investors" for speculators, whose gambling destabilizes global financial markets. We use the terms "money," "capital," "assets," and "wealth" interchangeably--leaving no simple means to differentiate money from real wealth. Money is a number. Real wealth is in food, fertile land, buildings, or other things that sustain us. Lacking language to see this difference, we accept the speculators' claim to "create wealth," when they expropriate it.

If in the 1980s we witnessed capitalism's triumph over communism, in the new millennium we may witness capitalism's triumph over life. For in the vocabulary of capitalism, the destruction of life to make money is progress.

When a defender of global capitalism asks, "What is your alternative? We've seen that central planning doesn't work," one can respond, "Adam Smith had a good idea. I favor a real market economy not centrally planned by governments or corporations." The vital distinction here is between the *market economy* Adam Smith had in mind, and the *capitalist economy,* which he would have abhorred.

In a healthy market economy, enterprises are human-scale and predominantly locally owned. People bring human sensibilities to bear on every aspect of economic life--resulting in self-organizing societies that maximize human freedom and minimize the need for coercive central control.

Capitalism, by contrast, is about using money to make money for people who have more than they need. It breeds inequality. Though capitalism cloaks itself in the rhetoric of democracy, it is dedicated to the elitist principle that sovereignty resides in property rather than in the person.

A real market economy creates real wealth. Global capitalism creates out-of-control speculation, which destroys real wealth.

- It depletes *natural capital* by strip-mining minerals, forests, and fisheries, and by dumping hazardous wastes that turn productive land and water into zones of death.

- It depletes *human capital* through substandard working conditions, as in the Mexican maquiladoras, where vital young women emerge after a few years with failed eyesight, allergies, and repetitive stress injuries that leave them permanency handicapped.

- It depletes social *capital* by uprooting factories on which communities depend--leaving society to absorb the family breakdown and violence that result.

- It depletes *institutional capital* by taking tax dollars through public subsidies and tax exemptions, and real wealth by weakening environmental standards essential to long-term societal health.

Living capital, which has the special capacity to regenerate itself, is the source of all real wealth. To destroy it for money--a number with no intrinsic value--is an act of collective insanity.

A real-world example of this insanity is the 1997 Asian financial crisis, in which a so-called "financial miracle" became a meltdown. That meltdown began in Thailand and spread through Malaysia, Indonesia, South Korea, and Hong Kong, as economies fell like dominoes. While specifics differed, the experience of Thailand reveals the underlying pattern.

During the "economic miracle" phase, large inflows of foreign money fueled rapidly growing financial bubbles in stock and real estate prices. (When too much money chases too few assets, those assets artificially "inflate" in price.) Those inflated bubbles attracted still more money, much of it from international banks eager to make loans to speculators, who secured loans with the inflated assets. As foreign currency poured in, consumers had the wherewithal to purchase imported goods, sales of which skyrocketed--creating the illusion of a booming economy.

Buying rapidly appreciating stocks or real estate seemed, for a time, a better deal than making productive investments in industry or agriculture. Ironically, the f aster foreign inv vestment flowed in, the more investments were sucked away from industry and agriculture and production stagnated or declined in both. Foreign financial obligations thus rose, while the capacity to repay those obligations fell. Once the speculators realized this was not sustainable, the meltdown began. Speculators pulled money out in anticipation of a crash, stock and real estate prices plummeted, and banks were left with uncollectable loans-- creating a liquidity crisis.

Capitalism can thus create an illusion of prosperity, even as it sets the stage for economic collapse. Lest we think this a rare example, we might note that since 1980, according to a McKinsey study, the financial assets of the world's largest economies have been growing at *two to three times* the rate of growth in gross domestic product (GDP). Bubbles are everywhere.

And it is in the nature of bubbles to pop because trading away life for money is not, in the long run, sustainable. Here's hoping we learn this lesson more gently than Asian economies have, but learn it we will. Squandering real wealth in the pursuit of numbers is ignorance of the worst kind. The potentially fatal kind.

Reading Set Number Four: The Nation-State

Problem: What is likely to be the role of armed conflict in the 21st century, and what is to be the likely role of the United States among global nation-states?

Exercise: Under what conditions do you believe it is appropriate for a nation-state to use violent force against its own citizens? Under what conditions is it appropriate for the nation-state to use violent force against the citizens of other countries?

The nation-state remains the major political force in the world. And few would argue that the United States is presently the predominant world power. But how much are these things likely to change in the next century? The article set in this section represents the thoughts about the political future of the United States from two of the most preeminent social historians of the 20th century, Eric Hobsbawm and Immanuel Wallerstein. Hobsbawm examines the patterns of area conflict in the 20th century to see what those patterns might tell us about armed conflict in the 21st century. He points out that while globalization has introduced many multilateral organizations to regulate and mediate world trade disputes, there is, as yet, no multilateral organization to settle armed conflicts. Furthermore, the nation-state has lost its monopoly on the use of armed force, as sophisticated weapon technology has become available to non-state groups, whose use of such weapons represents a challenge to the authority of nation-states. The 21st century, he concludes, will not be a century of peace.

In the second article Immanuel Wallerstein traces the emergence of the United States as the dominant global power. He then argues that, military dominance notwithstanding, U.S. dominance in world affairs will decline.

Study Questions 4

1. What were some of the major changes in the patterns of armed conflicts that occurred from the beginning to the end of the 2oth century?

2. What are some of the factors that are likely to dictate patterns of armed conflict in the 21st century?

3. What are the four symbols of the gradual decline of U.S. global hegemony?

4. What are some of the factors that will lead, according to Wallerstein, to the decline of U.S. global dominance?

Reading Number 1: War and peace by Eric Hobsbawm (The Guardian February 22 2002)

The 20th century was the most murderous in recorded history. The total number of deaths caused by or associated with its wars has been estimated at 187m, the equivalent of more than 10% of the world's population in 1913. Taken as having begun in 1914, it was a century of almost unbroken war, with few and brief periods without organized armed conflict somewhere. It was dominated by world wars: that is to say, by wars between territorial states or alliances of states.

The period from 1914 to 1945 can be regarded as a single "30 years' war" interrupted only by a pause in the 1920s - between the final withdrawal of the Japanese from the Soviet Far East in 1922 and the attack on Manchuria in 1931. This was followed, almost immediately, by some 40 years of cold war, which conformed to Hobbes's definition of war as consisting "not in battle only or the act of fighting, but in a tract of time wherein the will to contend by battle is sufficiently known". It is a matter for debate how far the actions in which US armed forces have been involved since the end of the cold war in various parts of the globe constitute a continuation of the era of world war. There can be no doubt, however, that the 1990s were filled with formal and informal military conflict in Europe, Africa and western and central Asia. The world as a whole has not been at peace since 1914, and is not at peace now.

Nevertheless, the century cannot be treated as a single block, either chronologically or geographically. Chronologically, it falls into three periods: the era of world war centered on Germany (1914 to 1945), the era of confrontation between the two superpowers (1945 to 1989), and the era since the end of the classic international power system. I shall call these periods I, II and III. Geographically, the impact of military operations has been highly unequal. With one exception (the Chaco war of 1932-35), there were no significant inter-state wars (as distinct from civil wars) in the western hemisphere (the Americas) in the 20th century. Enemy military operations have barely touched these territories: hence the shock of the bombing of the World Trade Center and the Pentagon on September 11.

Since 1945 inter-state wars have also disappeared from Europe, which had until then been the main battlefield region. Although in period III, war returned to south-east Europe, it seems very unlikely to recur in the rest of the continent. On the other hand, during period II inter-state wars, not necessarily unconnected with the global confrontation, remained endemic in the Middle East and south Asia, and major wars directly springing from the global confrontation took place in east and south-east Asia (Korea, Indochina). At the same time, areas such as sub-Saharan Africa, which had been comparatively unaffected by war in period I (apart from Ethiopia, belatedly subject to colonial conquest by Italy in 1935-36), came to be theatres of armed conflict during period II, and witnessed major scenes of carnage and suffering in period III.

Two other characteristics of war in the 20th century stand out, the first less obviously than the second. At the start of the 21st century we find ourselves in a world where armed operations are no longer essentially in the hands of governments or their authorized agents,   and where the contending parties have no common characteristics, status or objectives, except the willingness to use violence.

Inter-state wars dominated the image of war so much in periods I and II that civil wars or other armed conflicts within the territories of existing states or empires were somewhat obscured. Even the civil wars in the territories of the Russian empire after the October revolution, and those which took place after the collapse of the Chinese empire, could be fitted into the framework of international conflicts, insofar as they were inseparable from them. On the other hand, Latin America may not have seen armies crossing state frontiers in the 20th century, but it has been the scene of major civil conflicts: in Mexico after 1911, for instance, in Colombia since 1948, and in various central American countries during period II. It is not generally recognized that the number of international wars has declined fairly continuously since the mid-1960s, when internal conflicts became more common than those fought between states. The number of conflicts within state frontiers continued to rise steeply until it leveled off in the 1990s.

More familiar is the erosion of the distinction between combatants and non-combatants. The two world wars of the first half of the century involved the entire populations of belligerent countries; both combatants and non-combatants suffered. In the course of the century, however, the burden of war shifted increasingly from armed forces to civilians, who were not only its victims, but increasingly the object of military or military-political operations. The contrast between the first world war and the second is dramatic: only 5% of those who died in the first were civilians; in the second, the figure increased to 66%. It is generally supposed that 80 to 90% of those affected by war today are civilians. The proportion has increased since the end of the cold war because most military operations since then have been conducted not by conscript armies, but by small bodies of regular or irregular troops, in many cases operating high-technology weapons and protected against the risk of incurring casualties. There is no reason to doubt that the main victims of war will continue to be civilians.

It would be easier to write about war and peace in the 20th century if the difference between the two remained as clear-cut as it was supposed to be at the beginning of the century, in the days when the Hague conventions of 1899 and 1907 codified the rules of war. Conflicts were supposed to take place primarily between sovereign states or, if they occurred within the territory of one particular state, between parties sufficiently organized to be accorded belligerent status by other sovereign states. War was supposed to be sharply distinguished from peace, by a declaration of war at one end and a treaty of peace at the other. Military operations were supposed to distinguish clearly between combatants - marked as such by the uniforms they wore, or by other signs of belonging to an organized armed force - and non-combatant civilians. War was supposed to be between combatants. Non-combatants should, as far as possible, be protected in wartime.

It was always understood that these conventions did not cover all civil and international armed conflicts, and notably not those arising out of the imperial expansion of western states in regions not under   the jurisdiction of internationally recognized sovereign states, even though some (but by no means all) of these conflicts were known as "wars". Nor did they cover large rebellions against established states, such as the so-called Indian mutiny; nor the recurrent armed activity in regions beyond the effective control of the states or imperial authorities nominally ruling them, such as the raiding and blood-feuding in the mountains of Afghanistan or Morocco. Nevertheless, the Hague conventions still served as guidelines in the first world war. In the course of the 20th century, this relative clarity was replaced by confusion.

First, the line between inter-state conflicts and conflicts within states - that is, between international and civil wars - became hazy, because the 20th century was characteristically a century not only of wars, but also of revolutions and the break-up of empires. Revolutions or liberation struggles within a state had implications for the international situation, particularly during the cold war. Conversely, after the Russian revolution, intervention by states in the internal affairs of other states of which they disapproved became common, at least where it seemed comparatively risk-free. This remains the case.

Second, the clear distinction between war and peace became obscure. Except here and there, the second world war neither began with declarations of war nor ended with treaties of peace. It was followed by a period so hard to classify as either war or peace in the old sense that the neologism "cold war" had to be invented to describe it. The sheer obscurity of the position since the cold war is illustrated by the current state of affairs in the Middle East. Neither "peace" nor "war" exactly describes the situation in Iraq since the formal end of the Gulf war - the country is still bombed almost daily by foreign powers - or the relations between Palestinians and Israelis, or those between Israel and its neighbors, Lebanon and Syria. All this is an unfortunate legacy of the 20th-century world wars, but also of war's increasingly powerful machinery of mass propaganda, and of a period of confrontation between incompatible and passion-laden ideologies which brought into wars a crusading element comparable to that seen in religious conflicts of the past.

These conflicts, unlike the traditional wars of the international power system, were increasingly waged for non-negotiable ends such as "unconditional surrender". Since both wars and victories were seen as total, any limitation on a belligerent's capacity to win that might be imposed by the accepted conventions of 18th- and 19th- century warfare - even formal declarations of war - was rejected. So was any limitation on the victors' power to assert their will. Experience had shown that agreements reached in peace treaties could easily be broken.

In recent years the situation has been further complicated by the tendency in public rhetoric for the term "war" to be used to refer to the deployment of organized force   against various national or international activities regarded as anti-social - "the war against the Mafia", for example, or "the war against drug cartels". In these conflicts the actions of two types of armed force are confused. One - let's call them "soldiers" - is directed against other armed forces with the object of defeating them. The other - let's call them "police" - sets out to maintain or re-establish the required degree of law and public order within an existing political entity, typically a state. Victory, which has no necessary moral connotation, is the object of one force; the bringing to justice of offenders against the law, which does have a moral connotation, is the object of the other. Such a distinction is easier to draw in theory than in practice, however. Homicide by a soldier in battle is not, in itself, a breach of the law. But what if a member of the IRA regards himself as a belligerent, even though official UK law regards him as a murderer?

Were the operations in Northern Ireland a war, as the IRA held, or an attempt in the face of law-breakers to maintain orderly government in one province of the UK? Since not only a formidable local police force but a national army was mobilized against the IRA for 30 years or so, we may conclude that it was a war, but one systematically run like a police operation, in a way that minimized casualties and the disruption of life in the province. Such are the complexities and confusions of the relations between peace and war at the start of the new century. They are well illustrated by the military and other operations in which the US and its allies are at present engaged.

There is now, as there was throughout the 20th century, a complete absence of any effective global authority capable of controlling or settling armed disputes. Globalization has advanced in almost every respect - economically, technologically, culturally, even linguistically - except one: politically and militarily, territorial states remain the only effective authorities. There are officially about 200 states, but in practice only a handful count, of which the US is overwhelmingly the most powerful. However, no state or empire has ever been large, rich or powerful enough to maintain hegemony over the political world, let alone to establish political and military supremacy over the globe. A single superpower cannot compensate for the absence of global authorities, especially given the lack of conventions - relating to international disarmament, for instance, or weapons control - strong enough to be voluntarily accepted as binding by major states. Some such authorities exist, notably the UN, various technical and financial bodies such as the IMF, the World Bank and the WTO, and some international tribunals. But none has any effective power other than that granted to them by agreements between states, or thanks to the backing of powerful states, or voluntarily accepted by states. Regrettable as this may be, it isn't likely to change in the foreseeable future.

Since only states wield real power, the risk is that international institutions will be ineffective or lack universal legitimacy when they try to deal with offences such as "war crimes". Even when world courts are established by general agreement (for example, the International Criminal court set up by the UN Rome statute of July 17 1998), their judgments will not necessarily be accepted as legitimate and binding, so long as powerful states are in a position to disregard them. A consortium of powerful states may be strong enough to ensure that some offenders from weaker states are brought before these tribunals, perhaps curbing the cruelty of armed conflict in certain areas. This is an example, however, of the traditional exercise of power and influence within an international state system, not of the exercise of international law.

There is, however, a major difference between the 21st and the 20th century: the idea that war takes place in a world divided into territorial areas under the authority of effective governments which possess a monopoly of the means of public power and coercion has ceased to apply. It was never applicable to countries experiencing revolution, or to the fragments of disintegrated empires, but until recently most new revolutionary or post-colonial regimes - China between 1911 and 1949 is the main exception - emerged fairly quickly as more or less organized and functioning successor regimes and states. Over the past 30 years or so, however, the territorial state has, for various reasons, lost its traditional monopoly of armed force, much of its former stability and power, and, increasingly, the fundamental sense of legitimacy, or at least of accepted permanence, which allows governments to impose burdens such as taxes and conscription on willing citizens. The material equipment for warfare is now widely available to private bodies, as are the means of financing non-state warfare. In this way, the balance between state and non-state organizations has changed.

Armed conflicts within states have become more serious and can continue for decades without any serious prospect of victory or settlement: Kashmir, Angola, Sri Lanka, Chechnya, Colombia. In extreme cases, as in parts of Africa, the state may have virtually ceased to exist; or may, as in Colombia, no longer exercise power over part of its territory. Even in strong and stable states, it has been difficult to eliminate small, unofficial armed groups, such as the IRA in Britain and Eta in Spain. The novelty of this situation is indicated by the fact that the most powerful state on the planet, having suffered a terrorist attack, feels obliged to launch a formal operation against a small, international, non-governmental organization or network lacking both a territory and a recognizable army.

How do these changes affect the balance of war and peace in the coming century? I would rather not make predictions about the wars that are likely to take place or their possible outcomes. However, both the structure of armed conflict and the methods of settlement have been changed profoundly by the transformation of the world system of sovereign states.

The dissolution of the Soviet Union means that the Great Power system which governed international relations for almost two centuries and, with obvious exceptions, exercised some control over conflicts between states, no longer exists. Its disappearance has removed a major restraint on inter-state warfare and the armed intervention of states in the affairs of other states - foreign territorial borders were largely uncrossed by armed forces during the cold war. The international system was potentially unstable even then, however, as a result of the multiplication of small, sometimes quite weak states, which were nevertheless officially "sovereign" members of the UN.

The disintegration of the Soviet Union and the European communist regimes plainly increased this instability. Separatist tendencies of varying strength in hitherto stable nation-states such as Britain, Spain, Belgium and Italy might well increase it further. At the same time, the number of private actors on the world scene has multiplied. What mechanisms are there for controlling and settling such conflicts? The record is not promising. None of the armed conflicts of the 1990s ended with a stable settlement. The survival of cold war institutions, assumptions and rhetoric has kept old suspicions alive, exacerbating the post-communist disintegration of south-east Europe and making the settlement of the region once known as Yugoslavia more difficult.

These cold war assumptions, both ideological and power-political, will have to be dispensed with if we are to develop some means of controlling armed conflict. It is also evident that the US has failed, and will inevitably fail, to impose a new world order (of any kind) by unilateral force, however much power relations are skewed in its favor at present, and even if it is backed by an (inevitably shortlived) alliance. The international system will remain multilateral and its regulation will depend on the ability of several major units to agree with one another, even though one of these states enjoys military predominance.

How far international military action taken by the US is dependent on the negotiated agreement of other states is already clear. It is also clear that the political settlement of wars, even those in which the US is involved, will be by negotiation and not by unilateral imposition. The era of wars ending in unconditional surrender will not return in the foreseeable future.

The role of existing international bodies, notably the UN, must also be rethought. Always present, and usually called upon, it has no defined role in the settlement of disputes. Its strategy and operation are always at the mercy of shifting power politics. The absence of an international intermediary genuinely considered neutral, and capable of taking action without prior authorization by the Security Council, has been the most obvious gap in the system of dispute management.

Since the end of the cold war the management of peace and war has been improvised. At best, as in the Balkans, armed conflicts have been stopped by outside armed intervention, and the status quo at the end of hostilities maintained by the armies of third parties. Whether a general model for the future control of armed conflict can emerge from such interventions remains unclear.

The balance of war and peace in the 21st century will depend not on devising more effective mechanisms for negotiation and settlement but on internal stability and the avoidance of military conflict. With a few exceptions, the rivalries and frictions between existing states that led to armed conflict in the past are less likely to do so today. There are, for instance, comparatively few burning disputes between governments about international borders. On the other hand, internal conflicts can easily become violent: the main danger of war lies in the involvement of outside states or military actors in these conflicts.

States with thriving, stable economies and a relatively equitable distribution of goods among their inhabitants are likely to be less shaky - socially and politically - than poor, highly inegalitarian and economically unstable ones. The avoidance or control of internal armed violence depends even more immediately, however, on the powers and effective performance of national governments and their legitimacy in the eyes of the majority of their inhabitants. No government today can take for granted the existence of an unarmed civilian population or the degree of public order long familiar in large parts of Europe. No government today is in a position to overlook or eliminate internal armed minorities.

Yet the world is increasingly divided into states capable of administering their territories and citizens effectively and into a growing number of territories bounded by officially recognized international frontiers, with national governments ranging from the weak and corrupt to the non-existent. These zones produce bloody internal struggles and international conflicts, such as those we have seen in central Africa. There is, however, no immediate prospect for lasting improvement in such regions, and a further weakening of central government in unstable countries, or a further Balkanization of the world map, would undoubtedly increase the dangers of armed conflict.

A tentative forecast: war in the 21st century is not likely to be as murderous as it was in the 20th. But armed violence, creating disproportionate suffering and loss, will remain omnipresent and endemic - occasionally epidemic - in a large part of the world. The prospect of a century of peace is remote.

Reading Number 2: The Eagle Has Crash Landed by Immanuel Wallerstein (Foreign Policy, August 2002)

The United States in decline? Few people today would believe this assertion. The only ones who do are the U.S. hawks, who argue vociferously for policies to reverse the decline. This belief that the end of U.S. hegemony has already begun does not follow from the vulnerability that became apparent to all on September 11, 2001. In fact, the United States has been fading as a global power since the 1970s, and the U.S. response to the terrorist attacks has merely accelerated this decline. To understand why the so-called Pax Americana is on the wane requires examining the geopolitics of the 20th century, particularly of the century's final three decades. This exercise uncovers a simple and inescapable conclusion: The economic, political, and military factors that contributed to U.S. hegemony are the same factors that will inexorably produce the coming U.S. decline.

Intro to hegemony

The rise of the United States to global hegemony was a long process that began in earnest with the world recession of 1873. At that time, the United States and Germany began to acquire an increasing share of global markets, mainly at the expense of the steadily receding British economy. Both nations had recently acquired a stable political base—the United States by successfully terminating the Civil War and Germany by achieving unification and defeating France in the Franco-Prussian War. From 1873 to 1914, the United States and Germany became the principal producers in certain leading sectors: steel and later automobiles for the United States and industrial chemicals for Germany.

The history books record that World War I broke out in 1914 and ended in 1918 and that World War II lasted from 1939 to 1945. However, it makes more sense to consider the two as a single, continuous "30 years' war" between the United States and Germany, with truces and local conflicts scattered in between. The competition for hegemonic succession took an ideological turn in 1933, when the Nazis came to power in Germany and began their quest to transcend the global system altogether, seeking not hegemony within the current system but rather a form of global empire. Recall the Nazi slogan ein tausendjähriges Reich (a thousand-year empire). In turn, the United States assumed the role of advocate of centrist world liberalism—recall former U.S. President Franklin D. Roosevelt's "four freedoms" (freedom of speech, of worship, from want, and from fear)—and entered into a strategic alliance with the Soviet Union, making possible the defeat of Germany and its allies.

World War II resulted in enormous destruction of infrastructure and populations throughout Eurasia, from the Atlantic to the Pacific oceans, with almost no country left unscathed. The only major industrial power in the world to emerge intact—and even greatly strengthened from an economic perspective—was the United States, which moved swiftly to consolidate its position.

But the aspiring hegemon faced some practical political obstacles. During the war, the Allied powers had agreed on the establishment of the United Nations, composed primarily of countries that had been in the coalition against the Axis powers. The organization's critical feature was the Security Council, the only structure that could authorize the use of force. Since the U.N. Charter gave the right of veto to five powers—including the United States and the Soviet Union—the council was rendered largely toothless in practice. So it was not the founding of the United Nations in April 1945 that determined the geopolitical constraints of the second half of the 20th century but rather the Yalta meeting between Roosevelt, British Prime Minister Winston Churchill, and Soviet leader Joseph Stalin two months earlier.

The formal accords at Yalta were less important than the informal, unspoken agreements, which one can only assess by observing the behavior of the United States and the Soviet Union in the years that followed. When the war ended in Europe on May 8, 1945, Soviet and Western (that is, U.S., British, and French) troops were located in particular places—essentially, along a line in the center of Europe that came to be called the Oder-Neisse Line. Aside from a few minor adjustments, they stayed there. In hindsight, Yalta signified the agreement of both sides that they could stay there and that neither side would use force to push the other out. This tacit accord applied to Asia as well, as evinced by U.S. occupation of Japan and the division of Korea. Politically, therefore, Yalta was an agreement on the status quo in which the Soviet Union controlled about one third of the world and the United States the rest.

Washington also faced more serious military challenges. The Soviet Union had the world's largest land forces, while the U.S. government was under domestic pressure to downsize its army, particularly by ending the draft. The United States therefore decided to assert its military strength not via land forces but through a monopoly of nuclear weapons (plus an air force capable of deploying them). This monopoly soon disappeared: By 1949, the Soviet Union had developed nuclear weapons as well. Ever since, the United States has been reduced to trying to prevent the acquisition of nuclear weapons (and chemical and biological weapons) by additional powers, an effort that, in the 21st century, does not seem terribly successful.

Until 1991, the United States and the Soviet Union coexisted in the "balance of terror" of the Cold War. This status quo was tested seriously only three times: the Berlin blockade of 1948–49, the Korean War in 1950–53, and the Cuban missile crisis of 1962. The result in each case was restoration of the status quo. Moreover, note how each time the Soviet Union faced a political crisis among its satellite regimes—East Germany in 1953, Hungary in 1956, Czechoslovakia in 1968, and Poland in 1981—the United States engaged in little more than propaganda exercises, allowing the Soviet Union to proceed largely as it deemed fit.

Of course, this passivity did not extend to the economic arena. The United States capitalized on the Cold War ambiance to launch massive economic reconstruction efforts, first in Western Europe and then in Japan (as well as in South Korea and Taiwan). The rationale was obvious: What was the point of having such overwhelming productive superiority if the rest of the world could not muster effective demand? Furthermore, economic reconstruction helped create clientelistic obligations on the part of the nations receiving U.S. aid; this sense of obligation fostered willingness to enter into military alliances and, even more important, into political subservience.

Finally, one should not underestimate the ideological and cultural component of U.S. hegemony. The immediate post-1945 period may have been the historical high point for the popularity of communist ideology. We easily forget today the large votes for Communist parties in free elections in countries such as Belgium, France, Italy, Czechoslovakia, and Finland, not to mention the support Communist parties gathered in Asia—in Vietnam, India, and Japan—and throughout Latin America. And that still leaves out areas such as China, Greece, and Iran, where free elections remained absent or constrained but where Communist parties enjoyed widespread appeal. In response, the United States sustained a massive anticommunist ideological offensive. In retrospect, this initiative appears largely successful: Washington brandished its role as the leader of the "free world" at least as effectively as the Soviet Union brandished its position as the leader of the "progressive" and "anti-imperialist" camp.

One, Two, Many Vietnams

The United States' success as a hegemonic power in the postwar period created the conditions of the nation's hegemonic demise. This process is captured in four symbols: the war in Vietnam, the revolutions of 1968, the fall of the Berlin Wall in 1989, and the terrorist attacks of September 2001. Each symbol built upon the prior one, culminating in the situation in which the United States currently finds itself—a lone superpower that lacks true power, a world leader nobody follows and few respect, and a nation drifting dangerously amidst a global chaos it cannot control.

What was the Vietnam War? First and foremost, it was the effort of the Vietnamese people to end colonial rule and establish their own state. The Vietnamese fought the French, the Japanese, and the Americans, and in the end the Vietnamese won—quite an achievement, actually. Geopolitically, however, the war represented a rejection of the Yalta status quo by populations then labeled as Third World. Vietnam became such a powerful symbol because Washington was foolish enough to invest its full military might in the struggle, but the United States still lost. True, the United States didn't deploy nuclear weapons (a decision certain myopic groups on the right have long reproached), but such use would have shattered the Yalta accords and might have produced a nuclear holocaust—an outcome the United States simply could not risk.

But Vietnam was not merely a military defeat or a blight on U.S. prestige. The war dealt a major blow to the United States' ability to remain the world's dominant economic power. The conflict was extremely expensive and more or less used up the U.S. gold reserves that had been so plentiful since 1945. Moreover, the United States incurred these costs just as Western Europe and Japan experienced major economic upswings. These conditions ended U.S. preeminence in the global economy. Since the late 1960s, members of this triad have been nearly economic equals, each doing better than the others for certain periods but none moving far ahead.

When the revolutions of 1968 broke out around the world, support for the Vietnamese became a major rhetorical component. "One, two, many Vietnams" and "Ho, Ho, Ho Chi Minh" were chanted in many a street, not least in the United States. But the 1968ers did not merely condemn U.S. hegemony. They condemned Soviet collusion with the United States, they condemned Yalta, and they used or adapted the language of the Chinese cultural revolutionaries who divided the world into two camps—the two superpowers and the rest of the world.

The denunciation of Soviet collusion led logically to the denunciation of those national forces closely allied with the Soviet Union, which meant in most cases the traditional Communist parties. But the 1968 revolutionaries also lashed out against other components of the Old Left—national liberation movements in the Third World, social-democratic movements in Western Europe, and New Deal Democrats in the United States—accusing them, too, of collusion with what the revolutionaries generically termed "U.S. imperialism."

The attack on Soviet collusion with Washington plus the attack on the Old Left further weakened the legitimacy of the Yalta arrangements on which the United States had fashioned the world order. It also undermined the position of centrist liberalism as the lone, legitimate global ideology. The direct political consequences of the world revolutions of 1968 were minimal, but the geopolitical and intellectual repercussions were enormous and irrevocable. Centrist liberalism tumbled from the throne it had occupied since the European revolutions of 1848 and that had enabled it to co-opt conservatives and radicals alike. These ideologies returned and once again represented a real gamut of choices. Conservatives would again become conservatives, and radicals, radicals. The centrist liberals did not disappear, but they were cut down to size. And in the process, the official U.S. ideological position—antifascist, anticommunist, anticolonialist—seemed thin and unconvincing to a growing portion of the world's populations.

The Powerless Superpower

The onset of international economic stagnation in the 1970s had two important consequences for U.S. power. First, stagnation resulted in the collapse of "developmentalism"—the notion that every nation could catch up economically if the state took appropriate action—which was the principal ideological claim of the Old Left movements then in power. One after another, these regimes faced internal disorder, declining standards of living, increasing debt dependency on international financial institutions, and eroding credibility. What had seemed in the 1960s to be the successful navigation of Third World decolonization by the

United States—minimizing disruption and maximizing the smooth transfer of power to regimes that were developmentalist but scarcely revolutionary—gave way to disintegrating order, simmering discontents, and unchanneled radical temperaments. When the United States tried to intervene, it failed. In 1983, U.S. President Ronald Reagan sent troops to Lebanon to restore order. The troops were in effect forced out. He compensated by invading Grenada, a country without troops. President George H.W. Bush invaded Panama, another country without troops. But after he intervened in Somalia to restore order, the United States was in effect forced out, somewhat ignominiously. Since there was little the U.S. government could actually do to reverse the trend of declining hegemony, it chose simply to ignore this trend—a policy that prevailed from the withdrawal from Vietnam until September 11, 2001.

Meanwhile, true conservatives began to assume control of key states and interstate institutions. The neoliberal offensive of the 1980s was marked by the Thatcher and Reagan regimes and the emergence of the International Monetary Fund (IMF) as a key actor on the world scene. Where once (for more than a century) conservative forces had attempted to portray themselves as wiser liberals, now centrist liberals were compelled to argue that they were more effective conservatives. The conservative programs were clear. Domestically, conservatives tried to enact policies that would reduce the cost of labor, minimize environmental constraints on producers, and cut back on state welfare benefits. Actual successes were modest, so conservatives then moved vigorously into the international arena. The gatherings of the World Economic Forum in Davos provided a meeting ground for elites and the media. The IMF provided a club for finance ministers and central bankers. And the United States pushed for the creation of the World Trade Organization to enforce free commercial flows across the world's frontiers.

While the United States wasn't watching, the Soviet Union was collapsing. Yes, Ronald Reagan had dubbed the Soviet Union an "evil empire" and had used the rhetorical bombast of calling for the destruction of the Berlin Wall, but the United States didn't really mean it and certainly was not responsible for the Soviet Union's downfall. In truth, the Soviet Union and its East European imperial zone collapsed because of popular disillusionment with the Old Left in combination with Soviet leader Mikhail Gorbachev's efforts to save his regime by liquidating Yalta and instituting internal liberalization (perestroika plus glasnost). Gorbachev succeeded in liquidating Yalta but not in saving the Soviet Union (although he almost did, be it said).

The United States was stunned and puzzled by the sudden collapse, uncertain how to handle the consequences. The collapse of communism in effect signified the collapse of liberalism, removing the only ideological justification behind U.S. hegemony, a justification tacitly supported by liberalism's ostensible ideological opponent. This loss of legitimacy led directly to the Iraqi invasion of Kuwait, which Iraqi leader Saddam Hussein would never have dared had the Yalta arrangements remained in place. In retrospect, U.S. efforts in the Gulf War accomplished a truce at basically the same line of departure. But can a hegemonic power be satisfied with a tie in a war with a middling regional power? Saddam demonstrated that one could pick a fight with the United States and get away with it. Even more than the defeat in Vietnam, Saddam's brash challenge has eaten at the innards of the U.S. right, in particular those known as the hawks, which explains the fervor of their current desire to invade Iraq and destroy its regime.

Between the Gulf War and September 11, 2001, the two major arenas of world conflict were the Balkans and the Middle East. The United States has played a major diplomatic role in both regions. Looking back, how different would the results have been had the United States assumed a completely isolationist position? In the Balkans, an economically successful multinational state (Yugoslavia) broke down, essentially into its component parts. Over 10 years, most of the resulting states have engaged in a process of ethnification, experiencing fairly brutal violence, widespread human rights violations, and outright wars. Outside intervention—in which the United States figured most prominently—brought about a truce and ended the most egregious violence, but this intervention in no way reversed the ethnification, which is now consolidated and somewhat legitimated. Would these conflicts have ended differently without U.S. involvement? The violence might have continued longer, but the basic results would probably not have been too different. The picture is even grimmer in the Middle East, where, if anything, U.S. engagement has been deeper and its failures more spectacular. In the Balkans and the Middle East alike, the United States has failed to exert its hegemonic clout effectively, not for want of will or effort but for want of real power.

The Hawks Undone

Then came September 11—the shock and the reaction. Under fire from U.S. legislators, the Central Intelligence Agency (CIA) now claims it had warned the Bush administration of possible threats. But despite the CIA's focus on al Qaeda and the agency's intelligence expertise, it could not foresee (and therefore, prevent) the execution of the terrorist strikes. Or so would argue CIA Director George Tenet. This testimony can hardly comfort the U.S. government or the American people. Whatever else historians may decide, the attacks of September 11, 2001, posed a major challenge to U.S. power. The persons responsible did not represent a major military power. They were members of a nonstate force, with a high degree of determination, some money, a band of dedicated followers, and a strong base in one weak state. In short, militarily, they were nothing. Yet they succeeded in a bold attack on U.S. soil.

George W. Bush came to power very critical of the Clinton administration's handling of world affairs. Bush and his advisors did not admit—but were undoubtedly aware—that Clinton's path had been the path of every U.S. president since Gerald Ford, including that of Ronald Reagan and George H.W. Bush. It had even been the path of the current Bush administration before September 11. One only needs to look at how Bush handled the downing of the U.S. plane off China in April 2001 to see that prudence had been the name of the game.

Following the terrorist attacks, Bush changed course, declaring war on terrorism, assuring the American people that "the outcome is certain" and informing the world that "you are either with us or against us." Long frustrated by even the most conservative U.S. administrations, the hawks finally came to dominate American policy. Their position is clear: The United States wields overwhelming military power, and even though countless foreign leaders consider it unwise for Washington to flex its military muscles, these same leaders cannot and will not do anything if the United States simply imposes its will on the rest. The hawks believe the United States should act as an imperial power for two reasons: First, the United States can get away with it. And second, if Washington doesn't exert its force, the United States will become increasingly marginalized.

Today, this hawkish position has three expressions: the military assault in Afghanistan, the de facto support for the Israeli attempt to liquidate the Palestinian Authority, and the invasion of Iraq, which is reportedly in the military preparation stage. Less than one year after the September 2001 terrorist attacks, it is perhaps too early to assess what such strategies will accomplish. Thus far, these schemes have led to the overthrow of the Taliban in Afghanistan (without the complete dismantling of al Qaeda or the capture of its top leadership); enormous destruction in Palestine (without rendering Palestinian leader Yasir Arafat "irrelevant," as Israeli Prime Minister Ariel Sharon said he is); and heavy opposition from U.S. allies in Europe and the Middle East to plans for an invasion of Iraq.

The hawks' reading of recent events emphasizes that opposition to U.S. actions, while serious, has remained largely verbal. Neither Western Europe nor Russia nor China nor Saudi Arabia has seemed ready to break ties in serious ways with the United States. In other words, hawks believe, Washington has indeed gotten away with it. The hawks assume a similar outcome will occur when the U.S. military actually invades Iraq and after that, when the United States exercises its authority elsewhere in the world, be it in Iran, North Korea, Colombia, or perhaps Indonesia. Ironically, the hawk reading has largely become the reading of the international left, which has been screaming about U.S. policies—mainly because they fear that the chances of U.S. success are high.

But hawk interpretations are wrong and will only contribute to the United States' decline, transforming a gradual descent into a much more rapid and turbulent fall. Specifically, hawk approaches will fail for military, economic, and ideological reasons.

Undoubtedly, the military remains the United States' strongest card; in fact, it is the only card. Today, the United States wields the most formidable military apparatus in the world. And if claims of new, unmatched military technologies are to be believed, the U.S. military edge over the rest of the world is considerably greater today than it was just a decade ago. But does that mean, then, that the United States can invade Iraq, conquer it rapidly, and install a friendly and stable regime? Unlikely. Bear in mind that of the three serious wars the U.S. military has fought since 1945 (Korea, Vietnam, and the Gulf War), one ended in defeat and two in draws—not exactly a glorious record.

Saddam Hussein's army is not that of the Taliban, and his internal military control is far more coherent. A U.S. invasion would necessarily involve a serious land force, one that would have to fight its way to Baghdad and would likely suffer significant casualties. Such a force would also need staging grounds, and Saudi Arabia has made clear that it will not serve in this capacity. Would Kuwait or Turkey help out? Perhaps, if Washington calls in all its chips. Meanwhile, Saddam can be expected to deploy all weapons at his disposal, and it is precisely the U.S. government that keeps fretting over how nasty those weapons might be. The United States may twist the arms of regimes in the region, but popular sentiment clearly views the whole affair as reflecting a deep anti-Arab bias in the United States. Can such a conflict be won? The British General Staff has apparently already informed Prime Minister Tony Blair that it does not believe so.

And there is always the matter of "second fronts." Following the Gulf War, U.S. armed forces sought to prepare for the possibility of two simultaneous regional wars. After a while, the Pentagon quietly abandoned the idea as impractical and costly. But who can be sure that no potential U.S. enemies would strike when the United States appears bogged down in Iraq?

Consider, too, the question of U.S. popular tolerance of nonvictories. Americans hover between a patriotic fervor that lends support to all wartime presidents and a deep isolationist urge. Since 1945, patriotism has hit a wall whenever the death toll has risen. Why should today's reaction differ? And even if the hawks (who are almost all civilians) feel impervious to public opinion, U.S. Army generals, burnt by Vietnam, do not.

And what about the economic front? In the 1980s, countless American analysts became hysterical over the Japanese economic miracle. They calmed down in the 1990s, given Japan's well-publicized financial difficulties. Yet after overstating how quickly Japan was moving forward, U.S. authorities now seem to be complacent, confident that Japan lags far behind. These days, Washington seems more inclined to lecture Japanese policymakers about what they are doing wrong.

Such triumphalism hardly appears warranted. Consider the following April 20, 2002, New York Times report: "A Japanese laboratory has built the world's fastest computer, a machine so powerful that it matches the raw processing power of the 20 fastest American computers combined and far outstrips the previous leader, an I.B.M.-built machine. The achievement ... is evidence that a technology race that most American engineers thought they were winning handily is far from over." The analysis goes on to note that there are "contrasting scientific and technological priorities" in the two countries. The Japanese machine is built to analyze climatic change, but U.S. machines are designed to simulate weapons. This contrast embodies the oldest story in the history of hegemonic powers. The dominant power concentrates (to its detriment) on the military; the candidate for successor concentrates on the economy. The latter has always paid off, handsomely. It did for the United States. Why should it not pay off for Japan as well, perhaps in alliance with China?

Finally, there is the ideological sphere. Right now, the U.S. economy seems relatively weak, even more so considering the exorbitant military expenses associated with hawk strategies. Moreover, Washington remains politically isolated; virtually no one (save Israel) thinks the hawk position makes sense or is worth encouraging. Other nations are afraid or unwilling to stand up to Washington directly, but even their foot-dragging is hurting the United States.

Yet the U.S. response amounts to little more than arrogant arm-twisting. Arrogance has its own negatives. Calling in chips means leaving fewer chips for next time, and surly acquiescence breeds increasing resentment. Over the last 200 years, the United States acquired a considerable amount of ideological credit. But these days, the United States is running through this credit even faster than it ran through its gold surplus in the 1960s.

The United States faces two possibilities during the next 10 years: It can follow the hawks' path, with negative consequences for all but especially for itself. Or it can realize that the negatives are too great. Simon Tisdall of the Guardian recently argued that even disregarding international public opinion, "the U.S. is not able to fight a successful Iraqi war by itself without incurring immense damage, not least in terms of its economic interests and its energy supply. Mr. Bush is reduced to talking tough and looking ineffectual." And if the United States still invades Iraq and is then forced to withdraw, it will look even more ineffectual.

President Bush's options appear extremely limited, and there is little doubt that the United States will continue to decline as a decisive force in world affairs over the next decade. The real question is not whether U.S. hegemony is waning but whether the United States can devise a way to descend gracefully, with minimum damage to the world, and to itself.

Problem: To what extent are programs of population control ideologically driven as opposed to being concerned about the number of people. That is, to what extent are population control problems concerned more with the KIND of people increasing in the population as opposed to the number of people?

Exercise: If you were given the opportunity to engineer the physical and personality traits of your offspring, would you do it? If you would, which physical and personality traits would you choose?

Public policy is never ideologically neutral; that is, it contains assumptions that in one way or another favor the social, political, or economic interests of one group or another. Such is the case with population policy. Policies that address population growth inevitably contain assumptions about, not only the *number* of people that are desirable, but also the *kind* of people comprising a community or society. When people complain about overpopulation, often the concern is about the kind of people increasing in the population, as opposed to the absolute number. Generally, for example, if someone notes that a country or region is "overpopulated," you will find that the population density is less than most U.S. states, which are rarely described as "overpopulated."

Rarely acknowledged by population policy experts is the fact that population control originated with eugenic programs, policies to either prevent "undesirables" from reproducing or to "remove" undesirables from the population. British scientist Francis Galton first promoted the idea, reasoning that some British families (including his own) produced more people of intellectual accomplishments that others; therefore, it made sense to encourage those families to have more children while discouraging (legally if necessary) less accomplished people to have fewer. Galton's ideas gained wide acceptance (especially among those who assumed that they were favored), and eugenic control proposals were widely implemented, most notably in Germany in the Nazi era. However, while the rise and fall of Nazi Germany brought eugenics into disfavor, the basic ideas have never gone away, and have been resurrected with the advent of genetic engineering. The articles in this set of readings address the issue of the history of eugenics in the United States and Peru and describes the extent to which people went to weed out "undesirables" as a keystone of "population policy."

Study Questions 5

1. How does social Darwinism contribute to the doctrine of eugenics?

2. What was the general attitude of U.S. policy makers towards early eugenic efforts in Germany?

3. Under what kinds of programs were Andean villagers sterilized?

4. What sort of problems did sterilization programs create in Andean villages?

Reading Number 1: U.S. Eugenics Like Nazi Policy
Study: Forced Sterilizations Carried Out Longer Than Thought By David Morgan (Reuters, February 4, 2000)

U.S. doctors who once believed that sterilization could help rid society of mental illness and crime launched a 20th-century eugenics movement that in some ways paralleled the policies of Nazi Germany, researchers said today.

A Yale study tracing a once-popular scientific movement aimed at improving society through selective breeding indicates that state-authorized sterilizations were carried out longer and on a larger scale in the United States than previously believed, beginning with the first state eugenics law in Indiana in 1907.

Despite modern assumptions that American interest in eugenics waned during the 1920s, researchers said sterilization laws had authorized the neutering of more than 40,000 people classed as insane or "feebleminded" in 30 states by 1944.

Another 22,000 underwent sterilization between the mid-1940s and 1963, despite weakening public support and revelations of Nazi atrocities, according to the study, funded by the United States Holocaust Memorial Museum and the Merck Co. Foundation.

Forced sterilization was once legal in 18 U.S. states, and most states with eugenics laws allowed people to be sterilized without their consent by leaving the decision to a third party.

"The comparative histories of the eugenical sterilization campaigns in the United States and Nazi Germany reveal important similarities of motivation, intent and strategy," the study's authors wrote in the Annals of Internal Medicine, a journal published by the American College of Physicians-American Society of Internal Medicine.

Taking Social Darwinism Another Step

Eugenics sprang from the philosophy known as social Darwinism, which envisioned human society in terms of natural selection and suggested that science could engineer progress by attacking supposedly hereditary problems including moral decadence, crime, venereal disease, tuberculosis and alcoholism.

German and American eugenics advocates both believed science could solve social problems, tended to measure the worth of the individual in economic terms and felt mental illness a threat to society grave enough to warrant compulsive sterilization.

And while Nazi Germany's claims of Aryan superiority are well known, researchers said U.S. advocates of sterilization worried that the survival of old-stock America was being threatened by the influx of "lower races" from southern and eastern Europe.

There was also mutual admiration, with early U.S. policies drawing glowing reviews from authorities in pre-Nazi Germany.

"Germany is perhaps the most progressive nation in restricting fecundity among the unfit," editors of the New England Journal of Medicine wrote in 1934, a year after Hitler became chancellor.

'Better for All the World .'

But the study, based partly on old editorials from the New England Journal and the Journal of the American Medical Association, also demonstrated how the U.S. eugenics movement gradually waned while its Nazi counterpart carried out 360,000 to 375,000 sterilizations during the 1930s and grew to encompass so-called mercy killings.

"In the United States, a combination of public unease, Roman Catholic opposition, federal democracy, judicial review and critical scrutiny by the medical profession reversed the momentum," the article said.

The U.S. practice of neutering "mentally defective" individuals was backed by most leading geneticists and often justified on grounds that it would relieve the public of the cost of caring for future generations of the mentally ill.

Sterilizations also took place mainly in public mental institutions, where the poor and ethnic or racial minorities were housed in disproportionately high numbers.

"It is better for all the world, if instead of waiting to execute degenerate offspring for crime, or to let them starve for their imbecility, society can prevent those who are manifestly unfit from continuing their kind," Supreme Court Justice Oliver Wendell Holmes wrote in the majority opinion of a landmark eugenics case in 1926.

Reading Number 2: Peru Apologizes For At Least 200,000 Forced Sterilizations (United Press International, July 25, 2002)

Peru's Health Ministry issued a public apology following the publication of a report that revealed that the ministry oversaw a forced sterilization program during the presidency of Alberto Fujimori.

Health Minister Fernando Carbone confirmed that at least 200,000 Peruvians were sterilized without their consent or were persuaded to have the operation after officials bribed or threatened them.

The majority of the sterilizations took place between 1996 and 2000 in rural areas, particularly in the country's Andean region. The majority of victims were poor and frequently illiterate women from the Quechua and Aymara indigenous ethnic groups.

Several women are believed to have died after the operations, which often took place in unhygienic conditions. Only 45 percent of operations during the program were carried out under anesthesia, and the health authorities provided no aftercare.

One witness, Julia, told the investigating commission that a group of doctors visited her Andean village promising its residents a new era of well-being and improved health.

"Later they threatened us and practically forced us to do it (accept sterilization)," she said. "They shut me up in a room and forced me to get undressed. Everything that happened was because they used force. I didn't want to go through with it."

Julia also confirmed that because of the botched nature of the operation, she has a large scar across her stomach and is still in considerable pain.

Carbone announced legal proceedings Tuesday against those officials who designed and implemented the "attack on the physical and psychological integrity of these compatriots."

The minister said he hoped they would be swiftly brought to justice and would face severe punishment.

The report into the sterilization program suggests that just 10 percent of the 215,227 female sterilizations and 16,547 vasectomies carried out between 1996 and 2000 were voluntary.

The investigating commission said the remainder were either bullied into giving their permission by the Fujimori-era health authorities or were sterilized without their permission.

The figures for sterilizations are almost three times higher than in the period before the introduction of the program in 1996 and rose every year of the program as officials sought to meet Fujimori-imposed family-planning targets.

The program's focus on impoverished Andean villagers has created severe demographic problems in the region, and there is concern that a shortage of young people could threaten the future of traditional indigenous village life.

As well as interviewing victims of the program, the commission had access to 56 official documents, which they say proves the sterilization program was sanctioned at the highest levels of the Fujimori regime.

Carbone said there was no doubt that Fujimori knew about and approved the program.

"In the majority of cases we can see the clear influence of the presidential office as well as the involvement of senior state officials, including ministers and regional and general authorities," the minister said.

The revelations have led to calls for Fujimori to be charged with genocide. The former president is in voluntary exile in Japan. He fled Peru in 2000 in the wake of a major corruption scandal and is already wanted by the Peruvian authorities to face charges of treason and illegal enrichment.

Reading Set Number 6: Hunger and Poverty

Problem: How does one define poverty and what would it be like to be among the poorest 50% of the world's population?

Exercise: Suppose your annual income was $700 a year. You are married with two children. What sort of economic strategies would you devise to survive and how would you allocate your income. You must use prevailing prices for food, shelter, health care, clothing, etc.

For those of you living in one of the wealthiest countries of the world, it is hard to conceptualize the nature of poverty and what it would be like to grow up truly poor. Yet over half the world's population lives on less than the U.S. equivalent of $500 a year or less than $130 a year in a poor country. The two articles in this set describe some of the ways that we measure poverty and describe the effects of trying to live on an income well below what is necessary to sustain the basic necessities of life. The articles also document the extent to which income is uneven distributed and how most definitions of poverty are biased to show that free market capitalism has worked to reduce poverty.

Study Questions 6

1. What is Purchasing Power parity and how is it used to measure global poverty?

2. What evidence is there that global income inequality has increased over the past 20 years?

3. What is the difference in how poverty is measured in poor countries as opposed to how it is measured in rich countries?

4. Why, according to Michael Chossudovsky, are poverty statistics manipulated to show poverty reduction?

Reading Number 1: Global Poverty: The Gap Between the World's Rich and Poor Is Growing, and the Dying Continues by Thomas W. Pogge (Public Affairs Report. Vol. 42, No. 2, Summer 2001, University of California, Berkeley)

By far the most frequently unfulfilled human rights in our time are social and economic ones, such as everyone's right "to a standard of living adequate for the health and well-being of oneself and one's family, including food, clothing, housing, and medical care." Even with regard to global deficits in civil and political human rights, which are mainly concerned with the democratic exercise of power, due process, and the rule of law, poverty plays a decisive role.

Extremely poor people are often physically and mentally stunted due to malnutrition in infancy, unable even to read and write due to lack of schooling, and much preoccupied with their family's survival. They can cause little harm or benefit to the politicians and officials who rule them. Such rulers have little incentive to pay attention to the interests of the poor and cater instead to the interests of agents more capable of reciprocation, including foreign governments, companies, and tourists.

In describing global poverty, I will concentrate on (1) the extent of absolute poverty, how severe and widespread it is; (2) the extent of global inequality, which is a rough measure of the avoidability of poverty and the opportunity cost to the affluent of its avoidance; and (3) the trend of the first two aspects, that is, how global poverty and inequality tend to develop over time.

Let me summarize the state of our world in regard to these three aspects. The World Bank estimates that one fifth of all human beings—1.2 out of 6 billion—live below the international poverty line, which it currently defines in terms of $32.74 PPP 1993 per month or $1.08 PPP 1993 per day. PPP stands for purchasing power parity, so people count as poor by this standard when their income per person per year has less purchasing power than $393 had in the U.S. in 1993 or less than $466 have in the U.S. in the year 2000.

Those living below this poverty line fall, on average, 30 percent below it. So they live on $326 PPP 2000 per person per year on average. Now the $PPP incomes the World Bank ascribes to people in poor countries are on average about four times higher than their actual incomes at market exchange rates. Since virtually all the global poor live in such poor developing countries, we can estimate that their average annual *per capita* income of $326 PPP 2000 corresponds to about $82 at market exchange rates.

On average, the global poor can buy as much per person *per year* as we can buy with $326 in a rich country or with $82 in a poor country. These are the poorest of the poor. The World Bank provides statistics for a more generous poverty line that is twice as high: $786 PPP 1993 ($932 PPP or roughly $233 in the year

2000) per person per year. 2.8 billion people are said to live below this higher poverty line, falling 44.4 percent below it on average. This much larger group of people—nearly half of humankind—can then, on average, buy as much per person per year as we can buy with $518 in a rich country or with $130 in a poor one.

The consequences of such extreme poverty are foreseeable and extensively documented: 13 percent of the world's population (790 million) lack adequate nutrition, 17 percent (one billion) lack access to safe drinking water, 30 percent (over 2.4 billion) lack basic sanitation, approximately one billion adults are illiterate, 15 percent (more than 880 million) have no access to basic medical care, 17 percent (approximately one billion) lack adequate shelter, and 33 percent (2 billion) have no electricity.

Fully one third of all human deaths are due to poverty-related causes, such as starvation, diarrhea, pneumonia, measles, and malaria, which could be prevented or cured cheaply through food, safe drinking water, vaccinations, rehydration packs, or medicines. One quarter of all five to 14-year-olds work outside their family for wages, often under harsh conditions, in mining, textile and carpet production, prostitution, factories, and in agriculture.

Severe poverty is, of course, nothing new. What is new is the extent of global inequality. Real wealth is no longer limited to a small elite. Hundreds of millions enjoy a high standard of living with plenty of spare time, travel, education, cars, domestic appliances, computers, and so on. While average *per capita* annual income is about $82 in the bottom fifth (or quintile) and $131 among the bottom 46 percent of humankind, it is $26,000 in the so-called high-income economies consisting of 33 countries plus Hong Kong.

The collective income of the bottom quintile is about $100 billion annually or one third of one percent of the annual global product. The collective income of the bottom 46 percent is about $364 billion annually or 1.25 percent of the annual global product. By contrast, the high-income economies contain 14.9 percent of world population and control 78.4 percent of the global product. This contrast indicates what an economic reform bringing all incomes up to the World Bank's doubled poverty line would cost members of high-income economies: just over one percent of our income.

Global inequality is even greater in regard to property and wealth. Affluent people have on average more wealth than annual income, while the poor, on average, own significantly less than one annual income. The enormous fortunes of the super-rich in developed societies were given special emphasis in the penultimate *Human Development Report*: "The world's 200 richest people more than doubled their net worth in the four years to 1998, to more than $1 trillion. The assets of the top three billionaires are more than the combined GNP of all least developed countries and their 600 million people."

The last 50 years give the impression of rapid progress, punctuated by a long series of human rights declarations and treaties, new initiatives, summits, as well as detailed research into the quantification, causes, and effects of poverty. Such things are not unimportant. But they disguise the fact that real progress for the poor themselves is less impressive.

Yes, life expectancy has risen markedly in most countries and infant mortality has fallen substantially due to better disease control. But the number of people subsisting below the international poverty line has *increased* slightly since 1987, and has increased a lot when the special case of China is left aside. In the same period, the increase in the number of people living below the doubled poverty line is even more dramatic. And this despite the fact that this period has seen exceptional technological and economic progress as well as a dramatic decline in defense expenditures.

The number of malnourished people has likewise been basically flat at about 800 million—even though real prices of basic foodstuffs have fallen by 32 percent on average between 1985 and 2000. In the 13 years since the end of the Cold War, well over 200 million people, mostly children, have died from poverty-related causes.

While the trend in poverty and malnutrition is basically flat, the trend in global inequality, and hence in the avoidability of poverty, is dramatically negative: "The income gap between the fifth of the world's people living in the richest countries and the fifth in the poorest was 74 to 1 in 1997, up from 60 to 1 in 1990 and 30 to 1 in 1960. [Earlier] the income gap between the top and bottom countries increased from 3 to 1 in 1820 to 7 to 1 in 1870 to 11 to 1 in 1913." There is a long-established trend toward ever greater international income inequality—and this trend is accelerating: The figures just cited indicate an average annual growth gap of 1.66 percent for the colonial era (1820-1960), 2.34 percent for the period from 1960-90, and 3.00 percent for the period of 1990-97.

Think for a moment about how much ordinary Americans know about these facts. As the media presented retrospectives on the 20th century, they gave ample space to its human-made horrors: six million murdered in the German holocaust, 30 million starved to death in Mao's Great Leap Forward, 11 million wiped out by Stalin, two million killed by the Khmer Rouge, half a million hacked to death in Rwanda. When there are earthquakes, storms, and floods, we have them on the evening news, with footage of desperate parents grieving for their dead children.

What is not mentioned in the retrospectives and not shown on the evening news are the ordinary deaths from starvation and preventable diseases—some 200 million in just the few years since the end of the Cold War. Most of these 18 million dying each year are children whose parents simply cannot afford to give them access to safe water, nutritious food, vaccines, or basic medications. These deaths are not photogenic and quite disturbing, and we would rather not learn about them. So the media, ever catering to our tastes, leave them out. And the dying continues.

Reading Number 2: Global Falsehoods: How the World Bank and the UNDP Distort the Figures on Global Poverty by Michel Chossudovsky

Until the 1998 financial meltdown ("black September" 1998), the World economy was said to be booming under the impetus of the "free market" reforms.

Without debate or discussion, so-called "sound macro-economic policies" (meaning the gamut of budgetary austerity, deregulation, downsizing and privatization) continue to be heralded as the key to economic success and poverty alleviation. In turn, both the World Bank and the United Nations Development Programme (UNDP) have asserted authoritatively that economic growth in the late 20th Century has contributed to a reduction in the levels of World poverty. According to the UNDP, "the progress in reducing poverty over the 20th century is remarkable and unprecedented... The key indicators of human development have advanced strongly."

The Devastating Impacts of Macro-economic Reform are casually denied
The increasing levels of global poverty resulting from macro-economic reform are casually denied by G7 governments and international institutions (including the World Bank and the IMF); social realities are concealed, official statistics are manipulated, economic concepts are turned upside down.

The World Bank Methodology: Defining Poverty at a "Dollar a Day"
The World Bank framework deliberately departs from all established concepts and procedures (e.g. by the US Bureau of Census or the United Nations) for measuring poverty. It consists in arbitrarily setting a "poverty threshold" at one dollar a day per capita. It then proceeds (without even measuring) to deciding that population groups with a per capita income "above one dollar a day" are "non-poor".

The World Bank "methodology" conveniently reduces recorded poverty without the need for collecting country-level data. This "subjective" and biased assessment is carried out irrespective of actual conditions at the country level. The one dollar a day procedure is absurd: the evidence amply confirms that population groups with per capita incomes of 2, 3 or even 5 dollars a day remain poverty stricken (i.e. unable to meet basic expenditures of food, clothing, shelter, health and education).

Arithmetic Manipulation
Once the one dollar a day poverty threshold has been set (and "plugged into the computer"), the estimation of national and global poverty levels becomes an arithmetical exercise. Poverty indicators are computed in a mechanical fashion from the initial one dollar a day assumption.

"Authoritative" World Bank Numbers
These authoritative World Bank numbers are those which everybody quotes, --ie. 1.3 billion people below the poverty line. But nobody seems to have bothered to examine how the World Bank arrives at these figures.

The data is then tabulated in glossy tables with "forecasts" of declining levels of global poverty into the 21st Century. These World Bank "forecasts" of poverty are based on an assumed rate of growth of per capita income, --ie. growth of the latter implies pari passu a corresponding lowering of the levels of poverty. Its a numerical game!

World Bank "Forecasts": Poverty in China will decline to 2.9 percent by the Year 2000

According to the World Bank's "simulations", the incidence of poverty in China is to decline from 20 percent in 1985 to 2.9 percent by the year 2000. Similarly, poverty levels in India (where according to official data more than 80 percent of the population (1996) have per capita incomes below one dollar a day), the World Bank's "simulation" (which contradicts its own "one dollar a day" methodology) indicates a lowering of poverty levels from 55 percent in 1985 to 25 percent in the year 2000.

The whole framework (stemming from the one dollar a day assumption) is tautological; it is totally removed from an examination of real life situations. No need to analyze household expenditures on food, shelter and social services; no need to observe concrete conditions in impoverished villages or urban slums. In the World Bank framework, the "estimation" of poverty indicators has become numerical exercise.

The UNDP Framework

While the UNDP Human Development Group has in previous years provided the international community with a critical assessment of key issues of global development, the 1997 Human Development Report devoted to the eradication of poverty broadly conveys a similar viewpoint to that heralded by the Bretton Woods institutions. The UNDP's "human poverty index" (HPI) is based on "the most basic dimensions of deprivation: a short life span, lack of basic education and lack of access to public and private resources".

Based on the above criteria, the UNDP Human Development Group comes up with estimates of human poverty which are totally inconsistent with country-level realties. The HPI for Colombia, Mexico or Thailand, for instance, is of order of 10-11 percent (see Table 1). The UNDP measurements point to "achievements" in poverty reduction in Sub-Saharan Africa, the Middle East and India which are totally at odds with country-level data.

The human poverty estimates put forth by the UNDP portray an even more distorted and misleading pattern than those of the World Bank). For instance, only 10.9 percent of Mexico's population are categorized by the UNDP as "poor". Yet this estimate contradicts the situation observed in Mexico since the mid-1980s: collapse in social services, impoverishment of small farmers and the massive decline in real earnings triggered by successive currency devaluations. A recent OECD study confirms unequivocally the mounting tide of poverty in Mexico since the signing of the North American Free Trade Agreement (NAFTA).

Double Standards in the "Scientific" Measurement of Poverty

"Double standards" prevail in the measurement of poverty: the World Bank's one dollar a day criterion applies only to the "developing countries". Both the Bank and the UNDP fail to acknowledge the existence of poverty in Western Europe and North America. Moreover, the one dollar a day criterion is in overt contradiction with established methodologies used by Western governments and intergovernmental organizations to define and measure poverty in the "developed countries".

In the West, the methods for measuring poverty have been based on minimum levels of household spending required to meet essential expenditures on food, clothing, shelter, health and education. In the United States, for instance, the Social Security Administration (SSA) in the 1960s had set a "poverty threshold" which consisted of "the cost of a minimum adequate diet multiplied by three to allow for other expenses". This measurement was based on a broad consensus within the US Administration.

The US Poverty Threshold

The US "poverty threshold" for a family of four (two adults and two children) in 1996 was of the order of $16,036. This figure translates into a per capita income of eleven dollars a day (compared to the one dollar a day criterion of the World Bank used for developing countries). In 1996, 13.1 percent of the US population and 19.6 percent of the population in central cities of metropolitan areas were below the poverty threshold.

According to the UNDP Poverty in Mexico is lower than in the United States

Neither the UNDP nor the World Bank undertake comparisons in poverty levels between "developed" and "developing" countries. Comparisons of this nature would no doubt be the source of "scientific embarrassment" --ie. the poverty indicators presented by both organizations for Third World countries are in some cases of the same order of magnitude as (or even below) the official poverty levels in the US, Canada and the European Union. In Canada, heralded by the World community as "a promised land", occupying the first rank among all nations according to the same 1997 Human Development Report, 17.4 percent of the population are below the (official) poverty threshold compared to 10.9 percent for Mexico and 4.1 percent for Trinidad and Tobago.

Conversely, if the US Bureau of Census methodology (based on the cost of meeting a minimum diet) were applied to the developing countries, the overwhelming majority of the population would be categorized as "poor". While this exercise of using "Western standards" and definitions has not been applied in a systematic fashion, it should be noted that with the deregulation of commodity markets, retail prices of essential consumer goods are not appreciably lower than in the US or Western Europe. The cost of living in many Third World cities is higher than in the United States.

Moreover, household budget surveys for several Latin American countries suggest that at least sixty percent of the population the region does not meet minimum calorie and protein requirements. In Peru, for instance, following the

1990 IMF sponsored "Fujishock", 83 percent of the Peruvian population according to household census data were unable to meet minimum daily calorie and protein requirements. The prevailing situation in Sub-Saharan Africa and South Asia is more serious where a majority of the population suffer from chronic undernourishment.

The investigation on poverty by both organisations take official statistics at face value. It is largely an "office based exercise" conducted in Washington and New York with few insights or awareness of "what is happening in the field". The 1997 UNDP Report points to a decline of one third to a half in child mortality in selected countries of Sub-Saharan despite the slide in State expenditures and income levels. What it fails to mention, however, is that the closing down of health clinics and the massive lay-offs of health professionals (often replaced by semi-illiterate health volunteers) responsible for compiling mortality data has resulted in a de facto decline in recorded mortality. The IMF-World Bank sponsored macro-economic reforms have also led to a collapse in the process of data collection.

Vindicating the "Free" Market System
These are the realities which are concealed by the World Bank and UNDP poverty studies. The poverty indicators blatantly misrepresent country level situations as well as the seriousness of global poverty. They serve the purpose of portraying the poor as a minority group representing some 20 percent of World population (1.3 billion people).

Declining levels of poverty including forecasts of future trends are derived with a view to vindicating the "free market" policies and upholding the "Washington Consensus" on macro-economic reform. The "free market" system is presented as the "solution", namely as an instrument of poverty alleviation. The impacts of macro-economic reform are denied. Both institutions point to the benefits of the technological revolution and the contribution of foreign investment and trade liberalisation to the eradication of poverty.

Table 1
THE UNDP'S HUMAN POVERTY INDEX

Selected Developing Countries	Country Poverty Level (percent of the population below the poverty line)
Trinidad and Tobago	4.1
Mexico	10.9
Thailand	11.7
Colombia	10.7
Philippines	17.7
Jordan	10.9
Nicaragua	27.2
Jamaica	12.1
Iraq	30.7
Rwanda	37.9
Papua New Guinea	32.0
Nigeria	41.6
Zimbabwe	17.3

Source: Human Development Report 1997, table 1.1, p. 21

Table 2
POVERTY IN SELECTED G7 COUNTRIES, BY NATIONAL STANDARDS

Countries	Country Poverty Level (percent of the population below the poverty line)
United States (1996)*	13.7
Canada (1995)**	17.8
United Kingdom (1993)***	20.0
Italy (1993)***	17.0
Germany (1993)***	13.0
France (1993)***	17.0

*Source: *US Bureau of Census, ** Centre for International Statistics, Canadian Council on Social Development, ***European Information Service.*

Problem: How much is our lifestyle responsible for the degradation of the environment and are environmental problems best served by changing our lifestyle or by developing new technologies to fix environmental damage?

Exercise: Choose three food items that you normally have for breakfast and lunch and list the ingredients that go into each item. Then list the impacts on the environment that went into producing the food item. Don't forget to include the labor, the agricultural techniques, and the energy costs of production and distribution.

Few people dispute that the earth's environment has changed because of industrialization. However, not everyone agrees about what we should do about it. Much of the debate focuses on the extent of the damage being done, as well as on who is doing it. The debate over global warming and the Kyoto Protocol provides a good illustration. The Kyoto Protocol of 1992 called for countries to agree to limit their production of carbon-based gases whose release results in a gradual warming of the earth's surface temperature. While most countries have ratified the treaty in principal, the U.S. has not. Resistance comes largely from oil companies who fear reducing carbon emissions will reduce their profitability and from corporations who fear the costs of emission reduction. Some of even come up with their own "scientific" assessments that show global warming is not a problem or that carbon-emissions are actually beneficial. The articles in this set examine the debate over the environment, beginning with a brief article by Bjorn Lomborg who argues that that the environmental threat is vastly overblown and is followed by a report of talk by Nick Nichols on how corporations must resist pressure from so-called environmentalists. The set concludes with an article by Peter Montague who addresses issues raised by Lomborg while offering an assessment of the environment. Montague summarizes an environmental report of the Organization for Economic Cooperation and Development (OECD) that forecasts environmental trends in its 29 member countries, a forecast very different from that offered by Lomborg.

Study Questions 7

1. What evidence doe Bjorn Lomborg offer to show that environmental problems are not as severe as we think they are?

2. In what way does Lomborg argue that the costs of addressing global warming are far less than the benefits?

3. What are the arguments made by anti-environmentalists?

4. What are some of the solutions offered by Peter Montague for the problems of environmental degradation?

Reading Number 1: The Environmentalists Are Wrong By Bjorn Lomborg New York Times, August 26, 2002)

With the opening today of the United Nations World Summit on Sustainable Development in Johannesburg, we will be hearing a great deal about both concepts: sustainability and development. Traditionally, the developed nations of the West have shown greater concern for environmental sustainability, while the third world countries have a stronger desire for economic development. At big environmental gatherings, it is usually the priorities of the first world that carry the day.

The challenge in Johannesburg will be whether we are ready to put development ahead of sustainability. If the United States leads the way, the world may finally find the courage to do so.

Why does the developed world worry so much about sustainability? Because we constantly hear a litany of how the environment is in poor shape. Natural resources are running out. Population is growing, leaving less and less to eat. Species are becoming extinct in vast numbers. Forests are disappearing. The planet's air and water are getting ever more polluted. Human activity is, in short, defiling the earth — and as it does so, humanity may end up killing itself.

There is, however, one problem: this litany is not supported by the evidence. Energy and other natural resources have become more abundant, not less so. More food is now produced per capita than at any time in the world's history. Fewer people are starving. Species are, it is true, becoming extinct. But only about 0.7 percent of them are expected to disappear in the next 50 years, not the 20 percent to 50 percent that some have predicted. Most forms of environmental pollution look as though they have either been exaggerated or are transient — associated with the early phases of industrialization. They are best cured not by restricting economic growth but by accelerating it.

That we in the West are so prone to believe the litany despite the overwhelming evidence to the contrary results in an excessive focus on sustainability. Nowhere is this more pronounced than in the discussion on global warming.

There is no doubt that pumping out carbon dioxide from fossil fuels has increased the global temperature. Yet too much of the debate is fixated on reducing emissions without regard to cost. With its agreement to the 1997 Kyoto climate treaty, Europe has set itself the goal of cutting its carbon emissions to 1990 levels by 2012. This is more than 30 percent below what they would have been in 2012.

Even with renewable sources of energy taking over, the United Nations Climate Panel still estimates a temperature increase of four degrees to five degrees fahrenheit by the year 2100. Such a rise is projected to have less impact in the industrialized world than in the developing world, which tends to be in warmer regions and has an infrastructure less able to withstand the inevitable problems.

Despite our intuition that we need to do something drastic about global warming, economic analyses show that it will be far more expensive to cut carbon dioxide emissions radically than to pay the costs of adapting to the increased temperatures. Moreover, all current models show that the Kyoto Protocol will have surprisingly little impact on the climate: temperature levels projected for 2100 will be postponed for all of six years.

Yet the cost of the Kyoto Protocol will be $150 billion to $350 billion annually (compared to $50 billion in global annual development aid). With global warming disproportionately affecting third world countries, we have to ask if Kyoto is the best way to help them. The answer is no. For the cost of Kyoto for just one year we could solve the world's biggest problem: we could provide every person in the world with clean water. This alone would save two million lives each year and prevent 500 million from severe disease. In fact, for the same amount Kyoto would have cost just the United States every year, the United Nations estimates that we could provide every person in the world with access to basic health, education, family planning and water and sanitation services. Isn't this a better way of serving the world?

The focus should be on development, not sustainability. Development is not simply valuable in itself, but in the long run it will lead the third world to become more concerned about the environment. Only when people are rich enough to feed themselves do they begin to think about the effect of their actions on the world around them and on future generations. With its focus on sustainability, the developed world ends up prioritizing the future at the expense of the present. This is backward. In contrast, a focus on development helps people today while creating the foundation for an even better tomorrow.

The United States has a unique opportunity in Johannesburg to call attention to development. Many Europeans chastised the Bush administration for not caring enough about sustainability, especially in its rejection of the Kyoto Protocol. They are probably correct that the United States decision was made on the basis of economic self-interest rather than out of some principled belief in world development. But in Johannesburg the administration can recast its decision as an attempt to focus on the most important and fundamental issues on the global agenda: clean drinking water, better sanitation and health care and the fight against poverty.

Such move would regain for the United States the moral high ground. When United States rejected the Kyoto treaty last year, Europeans talked endlessly about how it was left to them to "save the world." But if the United States is willing to commit the resources to ensure development, it could emerge as the savior.

Reading Number 2: Corporations Urged Not To 'Appease' Environmental Groups By Marc Morano (CNSNews.com February 03, 2003)

American corporations were urged to stand up to environmental pressure groups and reject "appeasement" during a panel discussion at the Conservative Political Action Conference here on Saturday.

Nick Nichols, a crisis management expert and author of *The Rules for Corporate Warriors: How to Fight and Survive Attack Group Shakedowns* , said many companies believe that if they "give (environmental pressure groups) what they want maybe they will go away."

"They will not go away...appeasement didn't work with [former British Prime Minister] Neville Chamberlain when he tried it with [Adolf] Hitler," Nichols cautioned. Nichols made his remarks during a CPAC panel session called "Myth, Lies & Terror: The Growing Threat of Radical Environmentalism."

Nichols believes that many green groups have "nothing to do with bunnies or bambies" but instead are trying to eliminate "private property rights and force the rest of us to live our lives their way." Nichols compared the tactics of some environmental groups to a "protection racket."

In 1998 there were more than 4,000 tax-exempt environmental groups in the U.S. alone, and their assets were in excess of $8 billion dollars, according to Nichols.

"This is a big business folks...They are trying to convince the world that the U.S. is the devil incarnate," Nichols explained.

Nichols said his favorite rule for crisis management comes from a Smoky Mountains National Park Ranger who advised him how to avoid bear attacks in the wilderness.

"The most critical rule for survival in any situation is never look like food," Nichols recalled the park ranger advising.

"I thought that made a lot sense. A lot of [my] clients look like food to the more extreme environmental groups. Free enterprise, private property, the right to live where we want and purchase want we want is beginning to look like food," Nichols said.

'Home Grown Terrorists'

In an interview with **CNSNews.com,** Nichols spoke of the growing threat of eco-terrorism.

"The FBI estimates $50 million dollars of damage so far from 6,000 terrorist incidents by our home-grown terrorists," Nichols said.

"Government and industry have to start fighting these folks," he added. "It's time that the environmental extremists were forced to obey the law, it's time to challenge their tax exempt status."

Other panelists also took aim at the green groups. David Riggs, executive director of GreenWatch.org, a free-market environmental watchdog group, decried the environmentalists' "Deep Ecology" movement, which he describes as having an anti-human agenda.

"[Deep Ecology] puts human beings at the same level as any other species, [from] a grizzly bear to a virus. We humans are at the exact same level," Riggs explained.

George Landrith, president of Frontiers of Freedom, a free-market energy advocacy group, said the key to a healthy environment is wealth creation.

"Wealthier is healthier. Wealthier countries tend to have a far better environment than poorer countries," Landrith said.

Steve Milloy, publisher of JunkScience.com and author of *Junk Science Judo: Self Defense Against Health Scares and Scams* , told the panel that bad environmental science is permeating government studies on issues ranging from second-hand smoke to the chemical dioxin.

Citing several "junk science" studies done by the government, Milloy said, "Federal agencies need to do less science - they do a lousy job of science."

'They don't need more money, they need less money," he added.

Reading Number 3: Environmental Trends. By Peter Montague. (Rachel's Environment and Health News, #737 November 8, 2001)

Every couple of years someone writes a new report claiming that most environmental problems have been greatly exaggerated or don't even exist. There are now at least a dozen writers and publicists who spend their days putting a smiley face on environmental trends including Gregg Easterbrook (NEW REPUBLIC, and author, A MOMENT ON THE EARTH, 1995), Michael Fumento (author, SCIENCE UNDER SIEGE, 1993), Rush Limbaugh (syndicated radio talker), John Stossel (ABC TV), and John Tierney (NEW YORK TIMES), among others. Now a Danish mathematician, Bjorn Lomborg, has joined the ranks of these illuminati with a new book called THE OPTIMISTIC ENVIRONMENTALIST (2001), which we will review in the future.

The details vary, but the basic message from all these savants is similar: the environment is not seriously deteriorating; indeed, it is improving in almost every way. Human population? Growth has slowed. Forest loss? In many countries, tree cover is expanding. Global warming? It may not be so bad—northern winters will be more pleasant. Toxic chemicals? The worst is past. The real problem, they say, is all those gloomy environmentalists scaring us to death simply to raise money.

When these contrarian reports grab headlines, the public—understandably—doesn't know what to believe. Do environmental problems really exist or do they exist only in the minds of environmental wackos and professional doomsayers?

To get our bearings in this debate, we can turn to the mainstream of the mainstream: a new 327-page report titled OECD ENVIRONMENTAL OUTLOOK from the Organization for Economic Cooperation and Development, which describes environmental trends in the OECD's 29 member nations (Australia, Austria, Belgium, Canada, the Czech Republic, Denmark, Finland, France, Germany, Greece, Hungary, Iceland, Italy, Japan, Korea, Luxembourg, Mexico, the Netherlands, New Zealand, Norway, Poland, Portugal, the Slovak Republic, Spain, Sweden, Switzerland, Turkey, the U.K. and the U.S.).

This is no Chicken Little manifesto from the fringe.

The OECD report forecasts environmental trends to the year 2020, using a traffic signal to highlight major conclusions: green lights where things are improving and it's OK to "proceed with caution" (for example, organic agriculture, which is growing at 20% per year); yellow lights for big, important issues that are still shrouded in uncertainty (such as genetic engineering of food crops); and red lights for problems that require "urgent action" because they are likely to "significantly worsen" by 2020. (pg. 279) [Throughout this issue of RACHEL'S, page numbers refer to the OECD's ENVIRONMENTAL OUTLOOK report.]

Here is a bare-bones sketch of the most important "red light" problems that the OECD has identified:

** Human population, worldwide, will grow 1.1% per year between now and 2020, increasing from 6.1 billion people to 7.5 billion, or 23%. (pg. 40) This basic trend will impose a 23% greater burden on the natural environment in the next 20 years. Furthermore, as household size diminishes (requiring more individual homes) and urban sprawl increases, the burden imposed on the environment by each individual is steadily rising, the OECD says.

** Ocean fish provide 20% of all the protein in the human diet today (pg. 109) but 50% of the world's marine fisheries are already producing as much as they possibly can, 15% are being over-fished (an obviously unsustainable practice) and another 7% are fully depleted. Pressure on the oceans' fisheries will not decline any time soon because the global fishing fleet now has at least 30% more capacity than the oceans can supply on a sustained basis (pg. 113): more and more ships are chasing fewer and fewer fish. We should not expect increased fish yields from the oceans between now and 2020, the OECD says, so any increase must come from fish farming. But fish farms have serious problems of their own—large concentrations of fish-waste nutrients, which can deplete species diversity; large-scale feeding of antibiotics, which can harm other species and disturb whole ecosystems; and escaping fish that can drive out native species and spread disease. (pg. 115) As a consequence of these trends, the OECD forecasts a 10% decline in marine fish harvest by OECD countries by 2020. (pg. 112)

** Fresh water: The demand for fresh water must rise to keep pace with population growth, but water pollution is reducing the useable supply in most countries. As surface waters become exhausted or polluted, many countries begin pumping their underground aquifers, but nature replenishes such underground supplies only slowly. Seventeen countries are already pumping more water from underground than nature replaces each year. (pg. 102)

Furthermore, underground water supplies are being polluted:

"Available evidence suggests that there is a trend towards a worsening of aquifer water quality in OECD regions. Once groundwater sources are contaminated, they can be very difficult to clean up because the rate of flow is usually very slow and purification measures are often costly," the OECD says. (pg. 103) Worse, growing water scarcity is already giving rise to conflicts within and between countries, the OECD says, a trend likely to accelerate. (pg. 102)

** Forests: Within OECD countries, original "old growth" forests are being cut and replaced by secondary growth and by simple tree farms, which require artificial fertilizers and pesticides to survive. Thus, although the total area of forests is holding steady in OECD regions, the QUALITY of forested lands, in terms of natural habitat and biodiversity, is steadily declining. Some trees may grow quickly but forests take centuries to mature. The prospect for tropical forests is worse. With 37 million acres being cut down each year, "Tropical deforestation is expected to continue at alarming rates over the next few decades," says the OECD. (pg. 125) Between now and 2020, the world will lose almost 6% of its total forested land. (pg. 136)

** Acid Rain: Acid rain, snow and fog, caused by emissions of sulphur and nitrogen oxides, damage forests, soils and fresh water ecosystems. Acid rain "has been identified as an important factor in forest demise," says the OECD (pg. 127), and "Current acid deposition levels in Northern Europe and parts of North America are at least twice as high as critical levels." (pg. 190) In Europe the situation is expected to improve in the next 10 years but elsewhere in the world, it is expected to worsen. Outside OECD countries, both sulphur and nitrogen oxide emissions are expected to increase substantially in the next two decades:

"Thus, acid depositions are likely to continue to contribute to acidification of surface waters and soils in these areas and reduce the quality of the most sensitive ecosystems." (pg. 190)

** Biodiversity: Humans are relentlessly clearing and plowing up the habitat needed by other creatures, mostly converting it to farmland. Then many of the farmlands themselves are being despoiled by irrigation (which brings salts up from deep soils and deposits them in the top layers) and by soil erosion. According to the OECD, two-thirds of the world's farmlands have already been degraded to some degree and one-third have been "strongly or very strongly degraded." (pg. 138) Furthermore, half the world's wetlands have already been destroyed. (pg. 136) And the biodiversity of freshwater ecosystems is "under serious threat" with 20% of the world's fresh water fish extinct, threatened or endangered. (pg. 138) Half of all primates, and 9% of all known species of trees are at some risk of extinction, the OECD says. Between now and 2020, biodiversity in OECD countries is likely to degrade further. (pg. 138) It is hard to put a smiley face on the prognosis for biodiversity, the biological platform upon which all humans depend.

** Municipal solid waste, or garbage: In 1995, the average person in OECD countries created 1100 pounds of garbage each year. By 2020 this is expected to increase 28% to 1400 pounds per person per year. Because of growing population, total OECD garbage will increase 43% by 2020, reaching 847 million tons each year. (pgs. 203, 236) Outside the OECD regions, annual garbage production is expected to more than double by 2020, reaching 1450 million tons per year. (pg. 237)

In 1997, 64% of OECD garbage went to landfills (where it can contaminate underground water supplies [pg. 242]), 18% was incinerated (producing a range of noxious air pollutants, including the notoriously toxic, mobile and long-lived dioxins and furans [pg. 241]), and 18% was recycled. (pg. 235) By 2020, the OECD says, only 50% of OECD garbage will be landfilled, 17% will be incinerated, and 33% will be recycled. (pg. 240) Most waste ultimately escapes into the general environment in one form or another.

** Hazardous waste: OECD countries presently create 220 pounds of legally-hazardous waste per person per year. By 2020, per-capita production will rise 47% to 320 pounds per person per year and, because of growing population, total OECD hazardous waste will increase 60% to 194 million tons each year. (pgs. 137, 314) Significant portions of this will enter the general environment and eventually begin moving through food chains.

A partial survey of 13 out of 29 OECD countries has identified 475,000 sites that may be contaminated by hazardous industrial chemicals. The OECD estimates the cost of cleaning up these sites at $330 billion, a large number indeed. (pg. 242). . .

** Energy: Total energy use will increase 35% in OECD regions by 2020, and 51% elsewhere in the world. Oil will remain the OECD's energy mainstay, and the share of oil supplied by OPEC countries will increase from 54% today to 74% by 2020. Only 6% of energy will come from renewable sources (such as solar power) by 2020, says the OECD, and even this "will depend upon financial incentives from government." (pg. 148)

The OECD report does not say so, but any such financial incentives would be subject to challenge under World Trade Organization rules as illegal restraints of free trade. The WTO does not allow governments to subsidize particular industries, such as solar energy, though of course military subsidies to keep the oil flowing from the Middle East are allowed. By 2020, the share of OECD energy supplied by nuclear power may decline slightly from its current 11%, the OECD says, because the technology lacks popular support everywhere. (pg. 148)

** Global warming: "Global warming is a reality," says the OECD report. (pg. 157) As the Earth warms, we should expect more extreme weather in some regions (floods, droughts, and perhaps more "catastrophic" events such as large hurricanes and typhoons). We should also expect the sea level to rise somewhere between 6 inches and 37 inches by the year 2100, inundating valuable and densely-populated coastal lands. (pg. 162) Serious human diseases carried by mosquitoes, such as dengue fever (also called "breakbone fever" because it is so painful) and malaria, are likely to increase in both the northern and southern hemispheres, says the OECD. (pg. 162) "The possible effects of climate change are a widely recognized future threat to human health," says the OECD. "Climate change might result in new infectious diseases, as well as changing patterns of known diseases, and loss of life due to extreme weather conditions." (pg. 252)

"Overall studies show that some of the most adverse impacts [of global warming] are bound to occur in the Southern Hemisphere where countries are most vulnerable and least likely to easily adapt to climate change," says the OECD. (pg. 162)

Humans are contributing to global warming by releasing "greenhouse gases" -- mainly carbon dioxide, methane, and nitrous oxide. Of these, CO2 is the largest. The OECD forecasts CO2 emissions rising 33% in OECD countries and 100% in the rest of the world by 2020. To meet the goals of the Kyoto agreement, intended to curb the damage from global warming, OECD countries will need to reduce their CO2 emissions by anywhere from 18% to 40% depending on what non-OECD countries do. (pg. 160) Given that the U.S. increased its CO2 emissions 11% between 1990 and 1998, even an 18% reduction by 2020 would require a Herculean political commitment to reverse "business as usual." (pg. 159)

** Chemicals: Although the chemical industry creates large quantities of hazardous waste, an even bigger problem is its products. The OECD says there are somewhere between one and two million chemical preparations on the market today, each a mixture of two or more individual chemicals that do not react with each other. Each of these preparations must be considered in light of workplace hazards, accidents involving hazardous materials, and harmful exposures of workers in other industries, consumers, the general public, and the natural environment, says the OECD. Unfortunately, there is "an immense knowledge gap about chemicals on the market," says the OECD: governments "lack adequate safety information about the great majority of chemicals." (pg. 223) The "unknown hazard" from chemicals is a "major concern," says the OECD. (pg. 226)

"Major concerns exist about the possible impact on the environment and human health of substances produced by the chemicals industry, which are found in virtually every man-made product," says the OECD. "Many are being detected in the environment, where particular problems can be caused by persistent, bioaccumulative and toxic chemicals. Concern is growing, for example, about chemicals which cause endocrine disruption and which persist in the environment," OECD says. (pg. 223) Endocrine disruption refers to industrial chemicals, released into the environment, that interfere with the hormones that control growth, development, and behavior in all birds, fish, amphibians, reptiles, snails, lobsters, insects, and mammals, including humans.

Evidently the OECD does not have confidence that governments --or the chemical industry itself -- can control the chemical problem because the report explicitly says that vigilance by non-governmental organizations -- the environmental movement --will be "critical" to the success of efforts to assess the hazards of chemicals that are already on the market. (pg. 233) And of course assessing the hazards is only a first step --prelude to the much more contentious question of curbs, phase-outs, forced substitutions, or bans.

In sum, persistent toxic chemicals "are expected to continue being widespread in the environment over the next 20 years, causing serious effects on human health," the OECD says. (pg. 19)

** Human Health: "The loss of health due to environmental degradation is substantial" in OECD countries. (pg. 253) The "most urgent issues" are "air pollution and exposure to chemicals," the OECD says. The "greatest cause for concern" is the "threat of continuing widespread release of chemicals to the environment." (pg. 252) "This is not only a question of the amount of chemicals that end up in the environment, but more a question of their characteristics and effects. Unfortunately, the latter are often unknown, as the recent discovery of the endocrine disrupting effects of certain pesticide ingredients has shown," the OECD says. (pg. 252)

The OECD estimates that environmental degradation causes somewhere between 2% and 6% of all human disease in OECD countries and 8% to 13% in non-OECD countries. (pg. 250) In OECD countries this presently translates into health-care costs between $50 billion and $130 billion per year, the OECD says. (pg. 252)

The OECD report highlights two kinds of air pollution that can harm humans: ground-level ozone, and fine particles, both created by cars and trucks. Ground-level ozone -- a component of smog -- exacerbates asthma, bronchitis, emphysema and other chest ailments, and diminishes lung capacity even in healthy children. Health standards for ozone are exceeded at 95% of monitoring sites in the U.S. and Japan and at 90% of sites in Europe, the OECD reports. (pg. 188)

Fine particles -- soot so small that you can't see it, except as a haze -- presently kill twice as many people as automobile accidents each year, the OECD says. (pg. 176) And particles produced by diesel engines cause lung cancer -- in the U.S. alone, an estimated 125,000 new cases each year, the OECD says.

Environment and health costs from transportation presently amount to 8% of GDP (gross domestic product) in Europe, not counting the costs of traffic congestion, the OECD says. (pg. 176) And motor vehicles will increase 32% in OECD countries by 2020, and 74% worldwide. (pg. 170) As we approach 2020, stricter emission controls will reduce urban air contaminants in many OECD countries, but much of the rest of the world will be driving older cars and trucks without benefit of modern controls.

Environmentalists, of course, would like to add many details to the OECD's sobering report. The most blatant omission is the biggest killer of all -- the workplace environment. As we have reported previously, work-related injuries and disease kill about 165 workers EACH DAY in the U.S. alone -- a mammoth, ongoing human rights violation that the OECD report has managed to ignore. (See RACHEL'S #578.)

By cherry-picking data and sometimes fudging the details, writers like Bjorn Lomborg manage to confuse the public by claiming that environmental problems have been exaggerated or don't really exist. But this is the wrong time to be pretending that all is well because the trends are otherwise. The world's oceans, forests and biodiversity are clearly in trouble. Global warming is real and, given the political power of oil and coal companies, intractable. Waste is immense and growing, but toxic PRODUCTS are an even bigger problem. Toxic chemicals can now be measured at low levels in the bodies of living things everywhere on Earth, from the bottoms of the deepest oceans to the most remote mountain tops. Exotic industrial poisons have been introduced into all of us without our informed consent -- invading our bodies even before we are born -- and new harms from these toxic trespassers are discovered almost daily as ignorance and cover-up give way to openness and knowledge. But we needn't wait for yet another scientific study. We already know enough to act and act decisively.

The basic problem is that "free market" ideology regards the natural environment as an inexhaustible supermarket for raw materials and a bottomless free toilet for wastes. Both of these conceptions are dead wrong, and therefore "markets" must not be free -- they must be moderated by social covenants and government policies -- ranging from simple generosity and sharing on an international scale,

91

to fessing up and taking responsibility for the consequences of our actions on a corporate scale, plus a range of government sanctions and strictures, including purchasing preferences, subsidies for clean technologies, green taxes and fees, precautionary regulations and actions, guarantees of workplace safety and health (with real teeth), stiff fines, and even prison for repeat polluters. The key reforms must aim to create a vastly more responsive democracy, allowing people to make decisions by talking together about those things that affect their lives, displacing the elitist corporate rule that both Democrats and Republicans today call government.

Reversing environmental decline will require above all the commodity in shortest supply: courageous political commitment and democratic policy innovations based firmly and explicitly on the principle of forecaring or precaution, to counteract decades of "free market" theology that have left governments weakened, democracy vitiated, and the environment inadequately protected. If we and our unelected "leaders" can't -- or won't -- face up to the necessary changes, the environmental outlook for our children and grandchildren will be grim indeed.

Reading Set Number 8: Health and Disease

Problem: How are disease problems influenced by economic growth in wealthy countries? How can medicines and medical technologies developed in rich countries by drug companies be made available to people in poor countries?

Exercise: Drug companies argue that only if they are granted patent rights to products they develop, can the research they conduct be economically feasible. How does that argument hold up and are their alternative ways to both protect patent rights and provide access to medical advances to the poor?

People often assume that modern advances in health care will benefit all humanity. What is often ignored, however, is that like most other things in a market economy, health is a commodity that can be sold and is available only to people who can pay for it. Consequently there is a huge gap between availability of medicines and medical technologies in the rich countries of the global north as opposed to those in the south. This gap has been most evident in the case of HIV/AIDS medications. Anti-viral treatments for AIDS developed by drug companies cost $10,000-20,000 a year, effectively making them unavailable in countries most affected by the HIV/AIDS epidemic. When countries such as South Africa and Brazil began to make their own HIV/AIDS medicine based upon treatments developed by the drug companies, the companies appealed to the World Trade Organization charging that South Africa and Brazil were violating trade agreements that protected the monopolistic patents held by the companies. After broad condemnation, the drug companies backed down and agreed to make their treatments available at a reduced cost, although not as cheaply as the governments of South Africa and Brazil. The second article also reveals something of the attitudes of drug companies to customers in poorer countries. While it may be unfair to deduce that all drug companies behave the same, clearly the wealth gap between the global north and south has wide ramifications for global health. Unlike impoverished individuals who can be geographically marginalized within their own national boundaries, newly emergent diseases travel widely, often without detection.

Study Questions 8

1. What were some of the objections by health professionals for the wide-spread distribution if anti-viral HIV/AIDS drugs in poor countries?

2. What was the legal argument to support countries such as Brazil in their efforts to make cheap anti-viral HIV/AIDS drugs available to their citizens?

3. What were some of the reasons Bayer offered for its selling of more dangerous blood-clotting medicines to Asian and Latin American companies?

4. At what point did Bayer know about the dangers of its product, and when did they begin to alert customers?

Reading Number 1: Southern Sickness, Northern Medicine: Patently Wrong by Philippe Riviere (Le Monde Diplomatique, July 2001)

The Aids war began in South Africa. At the Durban world conference in June last year African sufferers denounced "medical apartheid" and called for universal access to anti-viral drugs. Most Aids victims are in the South, the medicines in the North. In Pretoria, on 19 April, 39 pharmaceutical companies that were suing the South African government took stock of the damage done to their image by their defiant defense of their patents and suddenly dropped proceedings. Their aim had been to show that South Africa's laws, designed to ensure an affordable supply of drugs to the country, contravened the Trips (trade-related aspects of intellectual property rights) agreements negotiated under the auspices of the World Trade Organization (WTO).

This about-turn would have been a fine victory. But the South African government then claimed it could not afford a large-scale program of medical care for Aids victims. "Anti-retrovirals are still expensive," explained health department spokeswoman Jo-Anne Collinge. Dr Bernard Pécoul of Médecins sans frontières (MSF) condemns this attitude. "In the Cape shantytown where 3m people live, a clinic set up by various organizations has been offering a program of prevention and screening for 18 months, which also allows opportunistic infections to be treated. In stark contrast to what the government says, we've been offering antiretrovirals since early May."

The donations and price cuts announced by the laboratories and described by French health minister Bernard Kouchner as tremendous sacrifices are, however, far from sufficient. Paying for treatment will require international mobilization on a new scale, to be headed up by United Nations secretary-general Kofi Annan. After four Security Council meetings devoted to the pandemic, he committed himself personally to setting up a global fund to fight Aids, tuberculosis and malaria.

Annan's initiative follows a proposal from a group of researchers and international experts gathered around economist Jeffrey Sachs at Harvard University, Boston. Noting the medical and moral failure of the international organizations in regard to Aids, they issued "a consensus statement on anti-viral treatments for Aids in poor countries" on 4 April that was widely reported in the international press.

Declarations of war

The Harvard document begins by arguing in favor of antiretroviral therapy:

despite its success in wealthy countries, it "remains largely inaccessible in the world's poorest countries, where interventions have focused almost exclusively on prevention. With soaring death rates from HIV/Aids in low-income countries, both the prevention of transmission of the virus and the treatment of those already infected must be global public health priorities."

The document refutes past objections such as "poor countries lack the adequate medical infrastructure to provide Aids treatment safely and effectively." It responds that some of the assistance provided will go to improving health care structures. Moreover, according to Dr Pécoul, experience in the Cape shantytown shows that, "unlike the white elephants proposed as pilot schemes by UNAids, quality treatment can be provided with modest resources."

A second objection was that "difficulties with adherence to complicated medication regimens would promote and spread drug resistance". Andrew Natsios of USAid, America's largest international development agency, goes so far as to say that many Africans "have never seen a clock or watch in their entire lives" and cannot be expected to take drugs at set hours of the day. If that is the case, why not also deny treatment to illiterate people in the North? This argument overlooks the fact that only a tiny minority of patients will be involved in such rigid drug regimens, those for whom treatments of first resort are not or have ceased to be effective.

The third objection was that paying for treatment would siphon resources away from prevention. But, the Harvard researchers stress, "appropriate treatment can not only prevent infected individuals from succumbing to life-threatening illness from Aids, but may play a major role in prevention both by reducing the viral load of those under treatment and by encouraging greater participation in prevention programs."

Targets have been proposed: 1m people undergoing treatment in three years' time (compared with 10,000 today). In its fifth year, the full program, prevention and treatment combined, would benefit 3m people and cost $6.3bn.

Access to drugs has suddenly become a viable proposition in international circles. In Pretoria the pharmaceutical companies are conceding defeat. Kofi Annan is looking to spend $7-10bn every year, which will come from governments, corporations and charitable foundations. Things are at last moving, hope returning.

But the small initial contribution announced by the United States in May ($200m, one tenth of the expected amount) has cast a shadow. And the conference held in Geneva on 4 June felt like a calling to order. The Global Fund, born of the need to finance access to treatment, seems to be turning its back on it, again focusing international solidarity on prevention alone. Dr David Nabarro, executive director at the office of Gro Harlem Brundtland, director-general of the World Health Organization (WHO), said there had been "an extraordinary degree of convergence" among delegates. The outcome of the debate was that victims will receive "a limited and carefully targeted amount of drug treatment".

Sachs believes this "drift of the Global Fund away from a balanced prevention-and-treatment strategy to a prevention-and-no-treatment focus would be a disaster. Prevention and treatment are an inseparable combination. The shocking underfunding of the effort so far can be no excuse for abandoning the cause of treatment. At least $7-10bn a year are needed for a serious effort. The underfunding of disease control remains one of the greatest acts of moral irresponsibility and political shortsightedness in the world today".

What good has come of these declarations of war by top international figures? "No war in the world is more important," General Colin Powell intoned during his visit to Kenya at the end of May. "I am the secretary of state of the United States of America, not the secretary of health, so why would I pay this kind of attention to this sort of an issue? This is more than a health issue. This is a social issue. This is a political issue. This is an economic issue. This is an issue of poverty".

Deal and counter-deal

The US National Security Council had previously identified the Aids epidemic as one of the greatest long-term threats to world stability. Apart from the health risk, the anticipated population imbalances will have drastic consequences beyond the borders of the countries concerned. What will become of a country where half the adult population is dying? What about the 13.2m Aids orphans?

But there was also an important legal issue that drove the new US administration to look at the matter again. President George W Bush's trade representative, Robert Zoellick, sees the controversy over access to drugs as an important test of the administration's broader drive to increase the adoption of free-trade principles in the US and around the world. He has voiced concern that a backlash is building against the drug industry for aggressively asserting its patent rights in the face of a monumental health crisis. He says: "The hostility that generates could put at risk the whole intellectual property rights system" (10).

A highly restrictive reading of the international agreements on industrial property has the effect of prohibiting the countries of the South from producing generic drugs; it also prevents the poorest of them from importing generics produced elsewhere at the lowest cost. But this interpretation is challenged by many organizations, including MSF, South Africa's Treatment Access Campaign and Act Up. They are lobbying governments, international organizations and in the streets for wider use of compulsory licenses and "parallel imports". The Trips agreement allows both these methods to be used in the event of a health emergency, for example.

Early this year the backlash occurred. Arraigned before the WTO by the US, Brazil mounted a forceful challenge against the financial burden of patents for its policy of making anti-Aids drugs available free of charge. On 25 June the US withdrew its complaint in exchange for a promise of talks before any compulsory license was granted in an American patent. Convergence is emerging in international forums between Brazil, India, Thailand and South Africa. France is timidly putting forward proposals. "We must explore other avenues, like producing new drugs in the developing countries themselves," President Jacques Chirac told the Durban conference on 9 July last year. Prime Minister Lionel Jospin took up the same point during a visit to South Africa this June. And the European communities are trying to take better account of public health imperatives in their interpretation of the Trips agreements (communication of 11 June 2001).

The Indian firm Cipla's offer to MSF to provide a cocktail of antiretrovirals for less than $350 a year (compared to the big boys' $10,000) resounded like a thunderbolt. Suddenly, the emergence in the South of very low cost generics producers seems credible.

James Love, coordinator of the Consumer Project on Technology in Washington and kingpin of the Cipla offer, stresses: "The success in the developing world of the southern producers is quite important. Otherwise there is no real leverage. It is important not to link use of the global fund to purchases from European and US producers, but rather, to permit competition and buy from the firms with the best price that have acceptable quality. Sachs has been terrible on this, urging purchases from big pharma exclusively."

Is that why the Harvard mechanism found favor with the Bush administration, the European Commission, the WHO experts, UNAids, the Bill and Melinda Gates Foundation and the pharmaceutical industry? It offered an answer to "medical apartheid" without dropping the guard on patents.

And yet, following Cipla, a lot of generics manufacturers have come on the scene, making treatments available for $200 a year. The Harvard formula would supply them for around $1000. "It would be extremely dangerous for the Global Fund to center around this deal between the pharmaceutical companies and the American administration," says Dr Pécoul. "An open reading of Article 30 of the Trips agreements would in fact allow the fund to purchase from the generics manufacturers. The total costs of drugs for 5m patients would then fall from $5bn to $1bn. That would resolve the prevention-treatment dilemma from the outset and release funds for infrastructure and patient follow-up."

In 1955 Dr Jonas Salk, creator of the first polio vaccine, was interviewed on television. When asked who the patent belonged to, he said: "Well, the people, I would say. There is no patent. Can you patent the sun?" At the end of his life Salk was devoting most of his work to the search for an Aids vaccine. Will his successors manage to shed a ray of sunshine in this present darkness?

Reading Number 2: 2 Paths of Bayer Drug in 80's: Riskier Type Went Overseas By Walt Bogdanich and Eric Koli (NY Times, May 22, 2003)

A division of the pharmaceutical company Bayer sold millions of dollars of blood-clotting medicine for hemophiliacs — medicine that carried a high risk of transmitting AIDS — to Asia and Latin America in the mid-1980's while selling a new, safer product in the West, according to documents obtained by The New York Times.

The Bayer unit, Cutter Biological, introduced its safer medicine in late February 1984 as evidence mounted that the earlier version was infecting hemophiliacs with H.I.V. Yet for over a year, the company continued to sell the old medicine overseas, prompting a United States regulator to accuse Cutter of breaking its promise to stop selling the product.

By continuing to sell the old version of the life-saving medicine, the records show, Cutter officials were trying to avoid being stuck with large stores of a product that was proving increasingly unmarketable in the United States and Europe.

Yet even after it began selling the new product, the company kept making the old medicine for several months more. A telex from Cutter to a distributor suggests one reason behind that decision, too: the company had several fixed-price contracts and believed that the old product would be cheaper to produce.

Nearly two decades later, the precise human toll of these marketing decisions is difficult, if not impossible, to document. Many patient records are now unavailable, and because an AIDS test was not developed until later in the epidemic, it is difficult to pinpoint when foreign hemophiliacs were infected with H.I.V. — before Cutter began selling its safer medicine or afterward.

But in Hong Kong and Taiwan alone, more than 100 hemophiliacs got H.I.V. after using Cutter's old medicine, according to records and interviews. Many have since died. Cutter also continued to sell the older product after February 1984 in Malaysia, Singapore, Indonesia, Japan and Argentina, records show. The Cutter documents, which were produced in connection with lawsuits filed by American hemophiliacs, went largely unnoticed until The Times began asking about them.

"These are the most incriminating internal pharmaceutical industry documents I have ever seen," said Dr. Sidney M. Wolfe, who as director of the Public Citizen Health Research Group has been investigating the industry's practices for three decades.

Bayer officials, responding on behalf of Cutter and its president at the time, Jack Ryan, declined to be interviewed but did answer written questions. In a statement, Bayer said that Cutter had "behaved responsibly, ethically and humanely" in selling the old product overseas.

Cutter had continued to sell the old medicine, the statement said, because some customers doubted the new drug's effectiveness, and because some countries were slow to approve its sale. The company also said that a shortage of plasma, used to make the medicine, had kept Cutter from manufacturing more of the new product.

"Decisions made nearly two decades ago were based on the best scientific information of the time and were consistent with the regulations in place," the statement said.

The medicine, called Factor VIII concentrate, essentially provides the missing ingredient without which hemophiliacs' blood cannot clot. By injecting themselves with it, hemophiliacs can stop bleeding or prevent bleeds from starting; some use it as many as three times a week. It has helped hemophiliacs lead normal lives.

But in the early years of the AIDS epidemic, it became a killer. The medicine was made using pools of plasma from 10,000 or more donors, and since there was still no screening test for the AIDS virus, it carried a high risk of passing along the disease; even a tiny number of H.I.V.-positive donors could contaminate an entire pool.

In the United States, AIDS was passed on to thousands of hemophiliacs, many of whom died, in one of the worst drug-related medical disasters in history. While admitting no wrongdoing, Bayer and three other companies that made the concentrate have paid hemophiliacs about $600 million to settle more than 15 years of lawsuits accusing them of making a dangerous product.

The Cutter documents — a few of them have surfaced in recent years in television and newspaper reports about Cutter's marketing practices — were gleaned from that litigation. But because the documents did not relate directly to the suits, most went uninvestigated.

The documents — internal memorandums, minutes of company marketing meetings and telexes to foreign distributors — reveal and chronicle Cutter's decision to keep exporting the older product after it began making the new one, which was heat-treated to kill H.I.V. The heat treatment rendered the virus "undetectable" in the product, according to a government study. (There are few available records documenting the actions and decisions of the three other American-based companies that also sold unheated concentrate after offering a heated product.)

Doctors and patients contacted overseas said they had not known of the contents of the Cutter documents. Bayer and other blood-product companies, though admitting no wrongdoing, have already made some payments to foreign hemophiliacs. It is unclear if Bayer could now face legal liability specifically for selling the older product after a safer one was available.

Federal regulators helped keep the overseas sales out of the public eye, the documents indicate. In May of 1985, believing that the companies had broken a voluntary agreement to withdraw the old medicine from the market, the Food and Drug Administration's regulator of blood products, Dr. Harry M. Meyer Jr., summoned officials of the companies to a meeting and ordered them to comply. "It was unacceptable for them to ship that material overseas," he said later in legal papers.

Even so, Dr. Meyer asked that the issue be "quietly solved without alerting the Congress, the medical community and the public," according to Cutter's account of the 1985 meeting. Dr. Meyer said later that he could not recall making that statement, but another blood-product company's summary of the meeting also noted that the F.D.A. wanted the matter settled "quickly and quietly." Dr. Meyer died in 2001.

Whether Cutter was behaving ethically became an issue in internal company discussions. "Can we in good faith continue to ship nonheat-treated coagulation products to Japan?" a company task force asked in February 1985, fearing that some of its plasma donors might be H.I.V. positive. The decision, records show, was yes.

Taken together, the documents provide an inside view of Cutter's bottom-line strategizing and efforts to manage the flow of information amid growing public anxiety about the safety of its product.

When a Hong Kong distributor in late 1984 expressed an interest in the new product, the records show, Cutter asked the distributor to "use up stocks" of the old medicine before switching to its "safer, better" product. Several months later, as hemophiliacs in Hong Kong began testing positive for H.I.V., some local doctors questioned whether Cutter was dumping "AIDS tainted" medicine into less-developed countries.

Still, Cutter assured the distributor that the unheated product posed "no severe hazard" and was the "same fine product we have supplied for years."

Li Wei-chun said her son, who died in 1996 at the age of 23, was one of the hemophiliacs in Hong Kong who got AIDS after using that product. "They did not care about the lives in Asia," Ms. Li said in a recent interview. "It was racial discrimination."

How It Started
Discovery That Blood Spreads the Disease

At the beginning of the epidemic, more than two decades ago, fear over what would later be known as AIDS was centered mostly among gays and intravenous drug users. But that changed on July 16, 1982, when the federal Centers for Disease Control reported that three hemophiliacs had acquired the disease.

This gave epidemiologists a strong reason to believe that the disease was being spread through blood products. And that belief carried grave implications for the many thousands of hemophiliacs who routinely injected themselves with concentrate made from giant pools of donated plasma.

Because an AIDS test had not yet been developed, federal health officials had no idea how many plasma donors carried the disease.

By March of 1983, the C.D.C. went so far as to warn that blood products "appear responsible for AIDS among hemophilia patients."

The unfolding story had not gone unnoticed at Cutter headquarters. Back in January, Cutter's manager of plasma procurement had acknowledged in a letter: "There is strong evidence to suggest that AIDS is passed on to other people through . . . plasma products."

With sales of concentrate beginning to slip, Cutter got more bad news in May 1983: after learning that a Cutter rival had begun to make heated concentrate, France decided to halt all imports of clotting concentrate until it could figure out what to do.

Fearing a loss of customers, Cutter conceived a marketing plan that stopped well short of full disclosure. "We want to give the impression that we are continuously improving our product without telling them we expect soon to also have a heat-treated" concentrate, an internal memo said.

Several weeks later, Cutter tried to minimize the danger hemophiliacs faced when using blood products. "AIDS has become the center of irrational response in many countries," the company said in a June 1983 letter to distributors in France and 20 other countries. "This is of particular concern to us because of unsubstantiated speculations that this syndrome may be transmitted by certain blood products."

The French decided to keep using unheated concentrate, and Cutter said it sold them more of the unheated product in August 1983. Later, two French health officials were sent to prison for continuing to use up old stocks of unheated concentrate in 1985, when a heated product was available.

Cutter finally received United States approval to sell heated concentrate on Feb. 29, 1984, the last of the four major blood product companies to do so. Though some doctors and patients held out against the heated product, a safer era had clearly begun for hemophiliacs in the United States.

Market Considerations
Bayer Says Some Wanted Old Product

For five months more, until August 1984, Cutter said it continued to make the old, unheated medicine. The records suggest that the company hoped to preserve the profit margin from "several large fixed-price contracts." But in its statements to The Times, Bayer also said that some customers still wanted the old medicine, initially believing — incorrectly, it turned out — that heating the concentrate could leave it less effective and possibly dangerous.

The new product, meanwhile, was selling briskly, leaving Cutter with a problem: "There is excess nonheated inventory," the company noted in minutes of a meeting on Nov. 15, 1984.

"They needed to get the return for what they invested," explained Michael Baum, a Los Angeles lawyer who has represented dozens of United States hemophiliacs in suits against blood-product companies. "They paid the donors. They had processed the plasma, put it into vials, kept it in warehouses — and all that expense had already been incurred." (One vial is roughly equivalent to a small dose, though more may be needed to stop severe bleeding.)

At the November meeting, the minutes show, Cutter said it planned to "review international markets again to determine if more of this product can be sold." And in the months that followed, it had some success, exporting more than 5 million units (a typical vial might contain 250 units) in the first three months of 1985, documents show.

"Argentina has been sold 300,000 units and will possibly order more, and the Far East has ordered 400,000 units," according to a March 1985 Cutter report. Two months later, the company reported that "in Taiwan, Singapore, Malaysia and Indonesia, doctors are primarily dispensing nonheated Cutter" concentrate.

By then, while there were still a small number of buyers in the United States, nearly all of the unheated concentrate was being sold abroad, available records show. All told, Cutter appears to have exported more than 100,000 vials of unheated concentrate, worth more than $4 million, after it began selling its safer product.

Gary Mull, an international product manager for Cutter at the time, said no one at the company had ordered him to sell the unheated concentrate as a way of avoiding a write-off. "If I had reason to personally believe, let alone the company" that any of the material was highly infectious, "we wouldn't have sent it out," he said.

Mr. Mull, who now works for another blood-product company, added, "I wasn't the shipping person, but I would still be the person in charge of queuing it up."

Bayer, which is based in Germany, said in its statement that an overall plasma shortage in 1985 had kept Cutter from making more heated medicine. But Cutter may actually have contributed to that shortage — by using some its limited plasma supplies to continue making the old product.

Bayer's response also emphasized that some countries were slow to approve its new product. For example, Bayer said "procedural requirements" imposed by Taiwan had delayed its "ability to apply for registration" and had led to other delays as well.

But an official at Taiwan's health department, Hsu Chien-wen, said recently that Cutter had not applied for permission to sell the new, safer medicine until July 1985, about a year and a half after it began doing so in the United States.

In one case, records show, Cutter officials even discussed trying to delay Japan's approval of heated concentrate so the company could shed stocks of the older product. Bayer said Cutter did not act on that idea.

Officials from the three other American-based companies that continued to sell unheated concentrate — Armour Pharmaceutical, Baxter International and Alpha Therapeutic — either declined to be interviewed or denied wrongdoing, in some cases citing the same reasons Bayer did for its decisions.

Still, what is not in dispute is that by the spring of 1985, few researchers doubted the connection between AIDS and unheated concentrate. The previous October, the federal Centers for Disease Control, using a prototype H.I.V. test, had reported that 74 percent of hemophiliacs who used unheated concentrate had tested positive for H.I.V. In the same report, the agency said a study done with Cutter had shown that heat treatment rendered the virus "undetectable."

(Bayer said no one knew "definitively" that its heat treatment killed the AIDS virus until eight months later.)

By May 1985, as the AIDS scare reached hemophiliacs in Hong Kong, Cutter's distributor there placed an urgent call to Cutter headquarters, records show. Sounding distraught, he told of an impending medical emergency. Hemophiliacs were frightened. Children were being infected with H.I.V. Parents were hysterical. Couldn't the company send the new, safer product?

Cutter replied that most of the new medicine was going to the United States and Europe, and that there was not enough left for Hong Kong, though a small amount was available for the "most vocal patients."

Dr. Chan Tai-kwong, who treated hemophiliacs at Queen Mary Hospital in Hong Kong, said doctors asked Cutter's distributor for the heated concentrate but could not get it; 40 percent of his patients were H.I.V.- positive, Dr. Chan said.

Dr. Patrick Yuen, who worked at another hospital, gave a similar account. "The local distributor asked us to keep using it," he said. "They said not to be afraid."

Even so, Cutter knew the market for the older medicine had all but dried up.

"It appears there are no longer any markets in the Far East where we can expect to sell substantial quantities of nonheat-treated," a Cutter official wrote in May 1985. Bayer said Cutter stopped shipping unheated concentrate in July 1985.

Later, in the early 1990's, two members of a Hong Kong government commission that concluded the tragedy could not have been avoided, expressed concern when told of the internal Cutter documents. Dr. Yuen, a member of the panel, said Cutter failed to warn doctors and hemophiliacs in Hong Kong about the dangers of unheated concentrate. "It should tell the whole world, not just Europe and America," he said.

Bayer also said Cutter did fully inform foreign customers about the heated product. And Bayer said it took more than a year to get Hong Kong's approval to sell it. But Dr. Cindy Lai, assistant director of Hong Kong's health department, said that in the 1980's Cutter needed only to get an import license. "It normally took one week," she said.

The delay harmed more than just the hemophiliacs, said Mrs. Li, the mother of the young hemophiliac who died of AIDS in 1993. Infected with a terrible and still mysterious disease, hemophiliacs were often shunned by family, friends and employers.

"It was the immoral drug company that caused some families to fall apart," she said. "They blamed and tortured each other. It was better to die than to live."

The Message Gap
Many Slow to Hear of the Problems

Today, in the Internet age, vast amounts of the most up-to-the-minute medical information are available at the click of a mouse. News moved less efficiently in 1985.

In Taiwan, Dr. Shen Ming-ching, who ran the country's largest clinic for hemophiliacs, recalled in a recent interview that it was not until he traveled to the United States for a conference in July 1985 that he learned for certain that heat treatment killed H.I.V. Upon returning home, he said, he immediately insisted that Taiwan authorities stop importing the old concentrate.

For his efforts on behalf of the hemophiliacs in Taiwan, Dr. Shen said, the government gave him a certificate and "a beautiful medal." As for the hemophiliacs themselves, 44 of Dr. Shen's patients got AIDS, including a 2-year-old. He said 23 had died.

None of the Taiwan patients interviewed by The Times said they knew that Cutter had begun selling the safer medicine in the United States in early 1984.

One Taiwan patient who received Cutter's old concentrate was Lee Ching-chang. Mr. Lee said he got his first concentrate in November 1983 at age 22, and continued receiving the unheated type into 1985.

Mr. Lee said he tested positive for H.I.V. in 1986. "I am bitterly angry," he said. Mr. Lee said he was too sick to work.

Six other hemophiliacs with H.I.V. or their families spoke to The Times about despair, discrimination, job loss or in some cases thoughts of suicide. Mr. Lee was the only hemophiliac with H.I.V. willing to be photographed.

Tang Fu-kuo helps AIDS patients in Taiwan. "I cannot tell myself that it's just history; let's forget it," Mr. Tang said. "Nobody wants to acknowledge fault."

Reading Set Number 9: Indigenous Peoples

Problem: What is lost as the culture of indigenous peoples is destroyed through the expansion of the culture of capitalism?

Exercise: What do you believe are the advantages of life in traditional cultures (such as that in Ladakh) over that of modern societies? What are some of the disadvantages?

The toleration of cultural diversity is not a strong point of the culture of capitalism. The nation-state, its dominant political form, requires at least the appearance of cultural uniformity. Furthermore, the cultures of indigenous peoples often clashes with the culture of capitalism: persons in indigenous societies often hold property in common, reducing or even precluding it being sold or traded. The mobility of many indigenous peoples necessitated by shifting agriculture or herding conflicts with the control needs of the nation-state. The kinship-based social organization often conflicts with the requirement for individual autonomy characteristic of the culture of capitalism. And indigenous societies tend to be far more egalitarian than societies of the culture of capitalism, reducing the needs of persons to assert their status through commodities. Finally, and perhaps most importantly, indigenous societies often control resources--land, mineral rights, intellectual resources--that are desired by members of the culture of capitalism. For these, among other reasons, indigenous cultures are fast disappearing, either through violent suppression and elimination, or through more subtle processes masked under the rubric of "modernization," "economic development," or "assimilation."

The readings in this set highlight the process of cultural devastation and what is lost through it. Helena Norberg-Hodge spent three decades trying to help people in the Himalayan province of Ladakh resist the destructive effects of modernization. In her article she first describes the richness of the traditional life of the people, dispelling the notion that traditional life was oppressive. She then outlines the process and the negative effects of modernization in Ladakh.

In the second article, Tom Goldtooth describes some aspects of indigenous spirituality and how it may contribute to a more protective attitude to our environment.

Study Questions 9

1. What were some of the effects of tourism in Ladakh?

2. Why do the people of Ladakh get a distorted image of life in modern society?

3. According to Tom Goldtooth, what is the difference in the view of the world promoted by globalization and that promoted by indigenous spirituality?

4. How does the view of the environment embedded in native spirituality promote a more protective attitude towards it?

Reading Number 1: The Pressure to Modernize and Globalize by Helena Norberg-Hodge (from The Case Against the Global Economy – And a Turn Toward the Local, edited by Jerry Mander and Edward Goldsmith, Sierra Club Books, 1996)

LADAKH is a high-altitude desert on the Tibetan Plateau in northernmost India. To all outward appearances, it is a wild and inhospitable place. In summer the land is parched and dry; in winter it is frozen solid by a fierce, unrelenting cold. Harsh and barren, Ladakh's land forms have often been described as a "moonscape."

Almost nothing grows wild — not the smallest shrub, hardly a blade of grass. Even time seems to stand still, suspended on the thin air. Yet here, in one of the highest, driest, and coldest inhabited places on Earth, the Ladakhis have for a thousand years not only survived but prospered. Out of barren desert they have carved verdant oases — terraced fields of barley, wheat, apples, apricots, and vegetables, irrigated with glacial meltwater brought many miles through stone-lined channels. Using little more than stone-age technologies and the scant resources at hand, the Ladakhis established a remarkably rich culture, one that met not only their material wants but their psychological and spiritual needs as well.

Until 1962, Ladakh, or "Little Tibet," remained almost totally isolated from the forces of modernization. In that year, however, in response to the conflict in Tibet, the Indian Army built a road to link the region with the rest of the country. With the road came not only new consumer items and a government bureaucracy but, as I shall show, a first misleading impression of the world outside. Then, in 1975, the region was opened up to foreign tourists, and the process of "development" began in earnest.

Based on my ability to speak the language fluently from my first year in Ladakh, and based on almost two decades of close contact with the Ladakhi people, I have been able to observe almost as an insider the effect of these changes on the Ladakhis' perception of themselves. Within the space of little more than a decade, feelings of pride gave way to what can best be described as a cultural inferiority complex. In the modern sector today, most young Ladakhis — the teenage boys in particular — are ashamed of their cultural roots and desperate to appear modern.

TOURISM

When tourism first began in Ladakh, it was as though people from another planet suddenly descended on the region. Looking at the modern world from something of a Ladakhi perspective, I became aware of how much more successful our culture looks from the outside than we experience it on the inside.

109

Each day many tourists would spend as much as $100—an amount roughly equivalent to someone spending $50,000 per day in America. In the traditional subsistence economy, money played a minor role and was used primarily for luxuries -- jewelry, silver, and gold. Basic needs -- food, clothing, and shelter were provided for without money. The labor one needed was free of charge, part of an intricate web of human relationships.

Ladakhis did not realize that money meant something very different for the foreigners; that back home they needed it to survive; that food, clothing, and shelter all cost money a lot of money. Compared to these strangers, the Ladakhis suddenly felt poor.

This new attitude contrasted dramatically with the Ladakhis' earlier self-confidence. In 1975, I was shown around the remote village of Hemis Shukpachan by a young Ladakhi named Tsewang. It seemed to me that all the houses we saw were especially large and beautiful. I asked Tsewang to show me the houses where the poor people lived. Tsewang looked perplexed a moment, then responded, "We don't have any poor people here."

Eight years later I overheard Tsewang talking to some tourists. "If you could only help us Ladakhis," he was saying, "we're so poor."

Besides giving the illusion that all Westerners are multimillionaires, tourism and Western media images also help perpetuate another myth about modern life — that we never work. It looks as though our technologies do the work for us. In industrial society today, we actually spend more hours working than people in rural, agrarian economies, but that is not how it looks to the Ladakhis. For them, work is physical work: ploughing, walking, carrying things. A person sitting behind the wheel of a car or pushing buttons on a typewriter doesn't appear to be working.

MEDIA IMAGES

Development has brought not only tourism but also Western and Indian films and, more recently, television. Together they provide overwhelming images of luxury and power. There are countless tools, magical gadgets, and machines — machines to take pictures, machines to tell the time, machines to make fire, to travel from one place to another, to talk with someone far away. Machines can do everything; it's no wonder the tourists look so clean and have such soft, white hands.

Media images focus on the rich, the beautiful, and the mobile, whose lives are endless action and glamour. For young Ladakhis, the picture is irresistible. It is an overwhelmingly exciting version of an urban American Dream, with an emphasis on speed, youthfulness, super-cleanliness, beauty, fashion, and competitiveness. "Progress" is also stressed: Humans dominate nature, while technological change is embraced at all costs.

In contrast to these utopian images from another culture, village life seems primitive, silly, and inefficient. The one-dimensional view of modern life becomes a slap in the face. Young Ladakhis whose parents ask them to choose a way of life that involves working in the fields and getting their hands dirty for very little or no money feel ashamed of their own culture. Traditional Ladakh seems absurd compared with the world of the tourists and film heroes.

This same pattern is being repeated in rural areas all over the South, where millions of young people believe contemporary Western culture to be far superior to their own. This is not surprising: looking as they do from the outside, all they can see is the material side of the modern world— the side in which Western culture excels. They cannot so readily see the social or psychological dimensions: the stress, the loneliness, the fear of growing old. Nor can they see environmental decay, inflation, or unemployment. This leads young Ladakhis to develop feelings of inferiority, to reject their own culture wholesale, and at the same time to eagerly embrace the global monoculture. They rush after the sunglasses, walkmans, and blue jeans not because they find those jeans more attractive or comfortable but because they are symbols of modern life.

Modern symbols have also contributed to an increase in aggression in Ladakh. Young boys now see violence glamorized on the screen. From Western-style films, they can easily get the impression that if they want to be modern, they should smoke one cigarette after another, get a fast car, and race through the countryside shooting people left and right.

WESTERN-STYLE EDUCATION

No one can deny the value of real education the widening and enrichment of knowledge. But today in the Third World, education has become something quite different. It isolates children from their culture and from nature, training them instead to become narrow specialists in a Westernized urban environment. This process has been particularly striking in Ladakh, where modern schooling acts almost as a blindfold, preventing children from seeing the very context in which they live. They leave school unable to use their own resources, unable to function in their own world.

With the exception of religious training in the monasteries, Ladakh's traditional culture had no separate process called education. Education was the product of a person's intimate relationship with the community and the ecosystem. Children learned from grandparents, family, and friends and from the natural world.

Helping with the sowing, for instance, they would learn that on one side of the village it was a little warmer, on the other side a little colder. From their own experience children would come to distinguish different strains of barley and the specific growing conditions each strain preferred. They learned how to recognize and use even the tiniest wild plant, and how to pick out a particular animal on a faraway mountain slope. They learned about connection, process, and change, about the intricate web of fluctuating relationships in the natural world around them.

For generation after generation, Ladakhis grew up learning how to provide themselves with clothing and shelter: how to make shoes out of yak skin and robes from the wool of sheep; how to build houses out of mud and stone. Education was location-specific and nurtured an intimate relationship with the living world. It gave children an intuitive awareness that allowed them, as they grew older, to use resources in an effective and sustainable way.

None of that knowledge is provided in the modern school. Children are trained to become specialists in a technological rather than an ecological society. School is a place to forget traditional skills and, worse, to look down on them.

Western education first came to Ladakhi villages in the 1970s. Today there are about two hundred schools. The basic curriculum is a poor imitation of that taught in other parts of India, which itself is an imitation of British education. There is almost nothing Ladakhi about it.

Once, while visiting a classroom in Leh, the capital, I saw a drawing in a textbook of a child's bedroom that could have been in London or New York. It showed a pile of neatly folded handkerchiefs on a four-poster bed and gave instructions as to which drawer of the vanity unit to keep them in. Many other schoolbooks were equally absurd and inappropriate. For homework in one class, pupils were supposed to figure out the angle of incidence that the Leaning Tower of Pisa makes with the ground. Another time they were struggling with an English translation of *The Iliad*.

Most of the skills Ladakhi children learn in school will never be of real use to them. In essence, they receive an inferior version of an education appropriate for a New Yorker, a Parisian, or a Berliner. They learn from books written by people who have never set foot in Ladakh, who know nothing about growing barley at 12,000 feet or about making houses out of sun-dried bricks.

This situation is not unique to Ladakh. In every corner of the world today, the process called *education* is based on the same assumptions and the same Eurocentric model. The focus is on faraway facts and figures, on "universal" knowledge. The books propagate information that is believed to be appropriate for the entire planet. But since the only knowledge that can be universally applicable is far removed from specific ecosystems and cultures, what children learn is essentially synthetic, divorced from its living context. If they go on to higher education, they may learn about building houses, but these "houses" will be the universal boxes of concrete and steel. So too, if they study agriculture, they will learn about industrial farming: chemical fertilizers and pesticides; large machinery and hybrid seeds. The Western educational system is making us all poorer by teaching people around the world to use the same global resources, ignoring those that the environment naturally provides. In this way, Western-style education creates artificial scarcity and induces competition.

In Ladakh and elsewhere, modern education not only ignores local resources but, worse still, robs children of their self-esteem. Everything in school promotes the Western model and, as a direct consequence, makes children think of themselves and their traditions as inferior.

Western-style education pulls people away from agriculture and into the city, where they become dependent on the money economy. Traditionally there was no such thing as unemployment. But in the modern sector there is now intense competition for a very limited number of paying jobs, principally in the government. As a result, unemployment is already a serious problem.

Modern education has brought some obvious benefits, such as improvement in the literacy rate. It has also enabled the Ladakhis to be more informed about the forces at play in the world outside. In so doing, however, it has divided Ladakhis from each other and the land and put them on the lowest rung of the global economic ladder.

LOCAL ECONOMY VERSUS GLOBAL ECONOMY

When I first came to Ladakh the Western macroeconomy had not yet arrived, and the local economy was still rooted in its own soils. Producers and consumers were closely linked in a community-based economy. Two decades of development in Ladakh, however, have led to a number of fundamental changes, the most important of which is perhaps the new dependence on food and energy from thousands of miles away.

The path toward globalization depends upon continuous government investments. It requires the buildup of a large-scale industrial infrastructure that includes roads, mass communications facilities, energy installations, and schools for specialized education. Among other things, this heavily subsidized infrastructure allows goods produced on a large scale and transported long distances to be sold at artificially low prices — in many cases at lower prices than goods produced locally. In Ladakh, the Indian government is not only paying for roads, schools, and energy installations but is also bringing in subsidized food from India's bread-basket, the Punjab. Ladakh's local economy which has provided enough food for its people for two thousand years is now being invaded by produce from industrial farms located on the other side of the Himalayas. The food arriving in lorries by the ton is cheaper in the local bazaar than food grown a five-minute walk away. For many Ladakhis, it is no longer worthwhile to continue farming.

In Ladakh this same process affects not just food but a whole range of goods, from clothes to household utensils to building materials. Imports from distant parts of India can often be produced and distributed at lower prices than goods produced locally — again, because of a heavily subsidized industrial infrastructure. The end result of the long-distance transport of subsidized goods is that Ladakh's local economy is being steadily dismantled, and with it goes the local community that was once tied together by bonds of interdependence.

Conventional economists, of course, would dismiss these negative impacts, which cannot be quantified as easily as the monetary transactions that are the goal of economic development. They would also say that regions such as the Punjab enjoy a "comparative advantage" over Ladakh in food production, and it therefore makes economic sense for the Punjab to specialize in growing food, while Ladakh specializes in some other product, and that each trade with the other. But when distantly produced goods are heavily subsidized, often in hidden ways, one cannot really talk about comparative advantage or, for that matter, "free markets," "open competition in the setting of prices," or any of the other principles by which economists and planners rationalize the changes they advocate. In fact, one should instead talk about the unfair advantage that industrial producers enjoy, thanks to a heavily subsidized infrastructure geared toward large-scale, centralized production.

In the past, individual Ladakhis had real power, since political and economic units were small, and each person was able to deal directly with the other members of the community. Today, "development" is hooking people into ever-larger political and economic units. In political terms, each Ladakhi has become one of a national economy of eight hundred million, and, as part of the global economy, one of about six billion.

In the traditional economy, everyone knew they had to depend directly on family, friends, and neighbors. But in the new economic system, political and economic interactions take a detour via an anonymous bureaucracy. The fabric of local interdependence is disintegrating as the distance between people increases. So too are traditional levels of tolerance and cooperation. This is particularly true in the villages near Leh, where disputes and acrimony within close-knit communities and even families have dramatically increased in the last few years. I have even seen heated arguments over the allocation of irrigation water, a procedure that had previously been managed smoothly within a cooperative framework.

As mutual aid is replaced by dependence on faraway forces, people begin to feel powerless to make decisions over their own lives. At all levels, passivity, even apathy, is setting in; people are abdicating personal responsibility. In the traditional village, for example, repairing irrigation canals was a task shared by the whole community. As soon as a channel developed a leak, groups of people would start shoveling away to patch it up. Now people see this work as the government's responsibility and will let a channel go on leaking until the job is done for them. The more the government does for the villagers, the less the villagers feel inclined to help themselves.

In the process, Ladakhis are starting to change their perception of the past. In my early days in Ladakh, people would tell me there had never been hunger. I kept hearing the expression *tungbos zabos:* "enough to drink, enough to eat." Now, particularly in the modern sector, people can be heard saying, "Development is essential; in the past we couldn't manage, we didn't have enough."

The cultural centralization that occurs through the media is also contributing both to this passivity and to a growing insecurity. Traditionally, village life included lots of dancing, singing, and theater. People of all ages joined in. In a group sitting around a fire, even toddlers would dance, with the help of older siblings or friends. Everyone knew how to sing, to act, to play music. Now that the radio has come to Ladakh, people do not need to sing their own songs or tell their own stories. Instead, they can sit and listen to the *best* singer, the *best* storyteller. As a result, people become inhibited and self-conscious. They are no longer comparing themselves to neighbors and friends, who are real people some better at singing but perhaps not so good at dancing — and they never feel themselves to be as good as the stars on the radio. Community ties are also broken when people sit passively listening to the very best rather than making music or dancing together.

ARTIFICIAL NEEDS

Before the changes brought by tourism and modernization, the Ladakhis were self-sufficient, both psychologically and materially. There was no desire for the sort of development that later came to be seen as a "need." Time and again, when I asked people about the changes that were coming, they showed no great interest in being modernized; sometimes they were even suspicious. In remote areas, when a road was about to be built, people felt, at best, ambivalent about the prospect. The same was true of electricity. I remember distinctly how, in 1975, people in Stagmo village laughed about the fuss that was being made to bring electric lights to neighboring villages. They thought it was a joke that so much effort and money was spent on what they took to be a ludicrous gain: "Is it worth all that bother just to have that thing dangling from your ceiling?"

More recently, when I returned to the same village to meet the council, the first thing they said to me was, "Why do you bother to come to our backward village where we live in the dark?" They said it jokingly, but it was obvious they were ashamed of the fact they did not have electricity.

Before people's sense of self-respect and self-worth had been shaken, they did not need electricity to prove they were civilized. But within a short period the forces of development so undermined people's self-esteem that not only electricity but Punjabi rice and plastic have become needs. I have seen people proudly wear wristwatches they cannot read and for which they have no use. And as the desire to appear modern grows, people are rejecting their own culture. Even the traditional foods are no longer a source of pride. Now when I'm a guest in a village, people apologize if they serve the traditional roasted barley, *ngamphe,* instead of instant noodles.

Surprisingly, perhaps, modernization in Ladakh is also leading to a loss of individuality. As people become self-conscious and insecure, they feel pressure to conform, to live up to the idealized images to the American Dream. By contrast, in the traditional village, where everyone wears the same clothes and looks the same to the casual observer, there seems to be more freedom to relax, and villagers can be who they really are. As part of a close-knit community, people feel secure enough to be themselves.

A PEOPLE DIVIDED

Perhaps the most tragic of all the changes I have observed in Ladakh is the vicious circle in which individual insecurity contributes to a weakening of family and community ties, which in turn further shakes individual self-esteem. Consumerism plays a central role in this whole process, since emotional insecurity generates hunger for material status symbols. The need for recognition and acceptance fuels the drive to acquire possessions that will presumably make you somebody. Ultimately, this is a far more important motivating force than a fascination for the things themselves.

It is heartbreaking to see people buying things to be admired, respected, and ultimately loved, when in fact the effect is almost inevitably the opposite. The individual with the new shiny car is set apart, and this furthers the need to be accepted. A cycle is set in motion in which people become more and more divided from themselves and from one another.

I've seen people divided from one another in many ways. A gap is developing between young and old, male and female, rich and poor, Buddhist and Muslim. The newly created division between the modern, educated expert and the illiterate, "backward" farmer is perhaps the biggest of all. Modernized inhabitants of Leh have more in common with someone from Delhi or Calcutta than they do with their own relatives who have remained on the land, and they tend to look down on anyone less modern. Some children living in the modern sector are now so distanced from their parents and grandparents that they don't even speak the same language. Educated in Urdu and English, they are losing mastery of their native tongue.

Around the world, another consequence of development is that the men leave their families in the rural sector to earn money in the modern economy. The men become part of the technologically based life outside the home and are seen as the only productive members of society. In Ladakh, the roles of male and female are becoming increasingly polarized as their work becomes more differentiated.

Women become invisible shadows. They do not earn money for their work, so they are no longer seen as "productive." Their work is not included as part of the Gross National Product. In government statistics, the 10 percent or so of Ladakhis who work in the modern sector are listed according to their occupations; the other 90 percent housewives and traditional farmers are lumped together as nonworkers. Farmers and women are coming to be viewed as inferior, and they themselves are developing feelings of insecurity and inadequacy.

Over the years I have seen the strong, outgoing women of Ladakh being replaced by a new generation women who are unsure of themselves and extremely concerned with their appearance. Traditionally, the way a woman looked was important, but her capabilities — including tolerance and social skills were much more appreciated.

Despite their new dominant role, men also clearly suffer as a result of the breakdown of family and community ties. Among other things, they are deprived of contact with children. When men are young, the new macho image prevents them from showing any affection, while in later life as fathers, their work keeps them away from home.

BREAKING THE BONDS BETWEEN YOUNG AND OLD

In the traditional culture, children benefited not only from continuous contact with both mother and father but also from a way of life in which different age groups constantly interacted. It was quite natural for older children to feel a sense of responsibility for the younger ones. A younger child in turn looked up to the older ones with respect and admiration and sought to be like them. Growing up was a natural, noncompetitive learning process.

Now children are split into different age groups at school. This sort of leveling has a very destructive effect: By artificially creating social units in which everyone is the same age, the ability of children to help and to learn from each other is greatly reduced. Instead, conditions for competition are automatically created, because each child is put under pressure to be just as good as the next one. In a group often children of quite different ages, there will naturally be much more cooperation than in a group of ten ck by the mutual respect and cooperation between Buddhists and Muslims. But within the last few years, growing competition has actually culminated in violence. Earlier there had been individual cases of friction, but the first time I noticed any signs of group tension was in 1986, when I heard Ladakhi friends starting to define people according to whether they were Buddhist or Muslim. In the following years, there were signs here and there that all was not well, but no one was prepared for what happened in the summer of 1989, when fighting suddenly broke out between the two groups. There were major disturbances in Leh bazaar, four people were shot dead by police, and much of Ladakh was placed under curfew.

Since then, open confrontation has died down, but mistrust and prejudice on both sides continue to mar relations. For a people unaccustomed to violence and discord, this has been a traumatic experience. One Muslim woman could have been speaking for all Ladakhis when she tearfully told me, "These events have torn my family apart. Some of them are Buddhists, some are Muslims, and now they are not even speaking to each other."

The immediate cause of the disturbances was the growing perception among the Buddhists that the Muslim-dominated state government was discriminating against them in favor of the local Muslim population. The Muslims for their part were becoming anxious that as a minority group they had to defend their interests in the face of political assertiveness by the Buddhist majority.

However, the underlying reasons for the violence are much more far-reaching. What is happening in Ladakh is not an isolated phenomenon. The tensions between the Muslims of Kashmir and the Hindu-dominated central government in Delhi; between the Hindus and the Buddhist government in Bhutan; and between the Buddhists and the Hindu government in Nepal, along with countless similar disturbances around the world, are, I believe, all connected to the same underlying cause: The intensely centralizing force of the present global development model is pulling diverse peoples from rural areas into large urban centers and placing power and decision making in the hands of a few. In these centers, job opportunities are scarce, community ties are broken, and competition increases dramatically. In particular, young men who have been educated for jobs in the modern sector find themselves engaged in a competitive struggle for survival. In this situation, any religious or ethnic differences quite naturally become exaggerated and distorted. In addition, the group in power inevitably tends to favor its own kind, while the rest often suffer discrimination.

Most people believe that ethnic conflict is an inevitable consequence of differing cultural and religious traditions. In the South, there is an awareness that modernization is exacerbating tensions; but people generally conclude that this is a temporary phase on the road to "progress," a phase that will only end once development has erased cultural differences and created a totally secular society. On the other hand, Westerners attribute overt religious and ethnic strife to the liberating influence of democracy. Conflict, they assume, always smoldered beneath the surface, and only government repression kept it from bursting into flames.

It is easy to understand why people lay the blame at the feet of tradition rather than modernity. Certainly, ethnic friction is a phenomenon that predates colonialism, modernization, and globalization. But after nearly two decades of firsthand experience on the Indian subcontinent, I am convinced that "development" not only exacerbates tensions but actually creates them. As I have pointed out, development causes artificial scarcity, which inevitably leads to greater competition. Just as importantly, it puts pressure on people to conform to a standard Western ideal blond, blue-eyed, "beautiful," and "rich" that is impossibly out of reach.

Striving for such an ideal means rejecting one's own culture and roots in effect, denying one's own identity. The inevitable result is alienation, resentment and anger. I am convinced that much of the violence and fundamentalism in the world today is a product of this process. In the industrialized world we are becoming increasingly aware of the impact of glamorous media and advertising images on individual self-esteem: problems that range from eating disorders such as anorexia and bulimia to violence over high-priced and "prestigious" sneakers and other articles of clothing. In the South, where the gulf between reality and the Western ideal is so much wider, the psychological impacts are that much more severe.

COMPARING THE OLD WITH THE NEW

There were many real problems in the traditional society, and development does bring some real improvements. However, when one examines the fundamentally important relationships — to the land, to other people, and to oneself— development takes on a different light. Viewed from this perspective, the differences between the old and the new become stark and disturbing. It becomes clear that the traditional nature-based society, with all its flaws and limitations, was more sustainable, both socially and environmentally. It was the result of a dialogue between human beings and their surroundings, a continuing co-evolution that meant that, during two thousand years of trial and error, the culture kept changing. Ladakh's traditional Buddhist worldview emphasized change, but that change occurred within a framework of compassion and a profound understanding of the interconnectedness of all phenomena.

The old culture reflected fundamental human needs while respecting natural limits. And it worked. It worked for nature, and it worked for people. The various connecting relationships in the traditional system were mutually reinforcing and encouraged harmony and stability. Most importantly, having seen my friends change so dramatically, I have no doubt that the bonds and responsibilities of the traditional society, far from being a burden, offered a profound sense of security, which seems to be a prerequisite for inner peace and contentment. I am convinced that people were significantly happier before development and globalism than they are today. The people were cared for, and the environment was well sustained — which criteria for judging a society could be more important?

By comparison, the new Ladakh scores very poorly when judged by these criteria. The modern culture is producing environmental problems that, if unchecked, will lead to irreversible decline; and it is producing social problems that will inevitably lead to the breakdown of community and the undermining of personal identity.

Reading Number 2: In the Native Way by Tom Goldtooth (Yes! A Journal of Positive Futures, Winter 2002)

Spirituality plays a very important role in the work our network does in environmental protection. It frames who we are. I believe that as Native people, we are the land and the land is us. Those of us in the environmental justice movement have started to educate the larger environmental movement that our work protecting the environment is spiritual work.

When we talk about the environment, very often we are talking about sacred elements. We're talking about air, which is a gift from the Creator. From the day that we're born, we take that first gasp of air and that's the life giver. Some day that breath of life is going to leave our body, thus completing its cycle.

Water is a sacred element. From the time the unborn is swimming around in the womb of its mother, we need water to sustain us. Throughout our lifetime, that water that flows through the veins of our Mother Earth remains connected to all life throughout the world.

The soil, the earth itself, that skin of Mother Earth is also one of the sacred elements.

And we have the sun that comes up in the morning every day that gives us warmth, that gives us the understanding. That's the fire, and fire is very sacred.

Some of the prophecies of our various tribes talk about a time when technology and development will be so far out of balance that it may affect the future of our planet. The Six Nations in the eastern Great Lakes area have prophecies about the time when the trees will start dying from the top down, and I understand that's happening. We've got glaciers in the Andes that are receding. We've got thinning ice in Alaska that is affecting the subsistence culture of the Alaska Natives. I hear that aquifers are starting to dry out. Climate change and global warming are impacting our people.

Our elders talk about the spiritual battle that's been going on for a long time. Industrialization has always wanted to control the land, control the people. That's going on today. I believe that globalization is part of that. Globalization places no value in people, no value in religious and spiritual principles, no value in the protection of the commons. Spiritual values tie us to the importance of protecting the Mother Earth, the plants, all animate and inanimate things. When we lose that understanding, industry, development, and globalization can do what they want to do, because there are no values behind their structures. Globalization has created a system of corporate ownership above the importance of plants, living things, and humans.

Back in the Old World—Europe—there were Crusades and Inquisitions, which did away with Earth-based religions. This practice rewrote history. Industrialization further killed off the Old World tribes, their identification, their traditional form of governance and replaced them with kingdoms and peasants. They've lost their connections to the land and who they are.

That's why I've always believed it's very important to carry on our traditions and our culture as Native peoples, to make sure our children know who they are and have that identification with the sacredness of our Mother Earth. Native peoples, especially those who are trying to practice ways that have been given to them since time immemorial, are an endangered species. Acculturation and assimilation—which are products of colonization—have been very effective. As Native peoples, we're still trying to hang on to what little we have left, our language, so we can practice our ceremonies, and our sacred areas. Western forms of development have gradually destroyed many of those sacred places.

The elders tell us that we're a tribal society of givers living in a society of takers. They say, "Go and do what you can to talk to people, try and educate them about these things." In the Native way, we respect people's own spirits. They have to come through their own self-realization to take responsibility for their actions.

A meeting of the tribes

Unfortunately, non-Native peoples no longer have traditional tribal systems, so we can't meet with them tribe to tribe. That was how we used to meet to deal with these kinds of issues. There were always ceremonial leaders, woman leaders, mechanisms for approaching these things. But that's not there anymore. Tribalism has been killed off.

As a practitioner of our traditional ways, I've been taught to put prayer first, to put the sacred Pipe first. These teachings provide me with the discipline to put the Creator first in everything I do. When I don't put the Creator first, then I start getting into trouble. I was taught that we're given a mind and a heart, and when we start to use the mind too much we get out of balance. We have to maintain a balance. Anytime I put prayer aside and try to do paperwork or do politics too much, I get myself in trouble.

In our traditional societies, we had political leaders, but political leaders maintained a balance with the spiritual leadership in the village. Various tribes had clan mothers or matrilineal clan systems that kept the menfolk in check. Our connection to the sacredness of the female creative principle of Mother Earth really means a lot, and that's something a lot of people don't understand. We always say that Mother Earth is sacred. She's the creative principle that allows life to go on, and that's why in our traditional values as Native peoples we have the most respect and reverence for the female. We're taught to take care of the Mother Earth and to take care of our women, our mothers, our aunts, our grandmothers, our sisters, our daughters in the same way we take care of the Earth.

I need to say that there are many different tribes and many different ways, but there are many similarities when I talk about the sacredness of Mother Earth and our relationship to the woman. Any time we start to lose that understanding, that's when we start getting into trouble as men.

Men have big egos. Men can easily lead religions and societies into warfare. That's why we always have to take direction from our women, from our matrilineal clan systems, because they understand the importance of that relationship. That was always the balance.

The men's role is also very important. The man is the protector of our villages and our women. I think that the men's and women's roles are out of balance in the same way that life is out of balance right now. I believe that men have to somehow find out what our role is in the modern world. The woman still carries forth the children, still understands that creative principle, still has that connection to the Earth and the powers of the moon. Their role is more easily defined. But I find a lot of brothers, no matter what race, are out of balance, searching to find out who they are as a man. We must not forget that Father Sky and Mother Earth need one another as part of the creative principle.

That goes back to the work that we do with the environment. When I talk to white environmentalists about the importance of the spiritual aspects of their work, they have no understanding of that—especially the men. The women seem to have a better understanding. Very often, the closest the non-Natives can understand about the sacredness of the Earth is the concept of stewardship—which is good but still has ownership attached to it. But we can work with stewardship as a beginning.

Sharing ceremonies

A lot of the prophecies of the various tribes have said the time will come when the younger brother and the younger sister who have come from across the ocean will start to look towards the Native peoples for direction. But in my younger years, I was very resistant to the new agers coming into our lands and into our ceremonies.

My youth led me into Native activism—what we called Red Power. I was one of those foot soldiers demanding the recognition of our treaty rights with my fists in the air, demanding justice. I talked to my grandmother once, and she said, "You've got a lot of anger in you. What's wrong?" So I started talking about what was going on, about people being killed. She said, "You need to go into ceremony. You've got a lot of anger."

As the years went on, I started to see more non-Native people, basically white people, coming to our ceremonies looking for answers, and I struggled with that. It seemed to me they were continuing the same old practice of taking things away from us without giving back. Now it was our ceremony and knowledge.

An uncle on the Dakota Reservation in Prairie Island, Minnesota, asked me to help him in the sweat lodge in the mid-1980s. He had a dream that the four colors of man would be coming to his ceremonies. Sure enough, soon people started coming down from the Twin Cities on Friday nights, carloads of them, and there I was helping him with all these people. I wouldn't have done it if he hadn't asked. But he needed help; he was getting tired. I really had to work this out for myself, because I couldn't take my anger into the sweat lodge. I started to learn about compassion.

I feel people in this country as well as in Europe are searching. I've been to a German sweat lodge, which was given to them by a full-blood Cherokee man in the '70s. In 2000 in Germany I was sitting in the sweat lodge with these German people. They said they had lost their ways from the Crusades a long time ago, and this Native sweat lodge was all they had to help them make their way back to who they were. I saw they had respect and humility about these spiritual ways. They demonstrated compassion for each other, love, and faith in the Higher Power—they have everything that we need to live and survive. Who's to say that what they're doing is wrong? I started to see that this spiritual understanding is to be shared with all people, regardless of race.

Back in the 1980s, I met some people with the Rainbow tribe. The Rainbow tribe is mostly white folks, but there are some black people, Latinos, and Asians. I had my own stereotypes about the Rainbow tribe—basically hippie-type folks who smoked marijuana, partied, and tried to have a connection with the Earth. I thought there was something out of balance, and I usually stayed away from the Rainbow gatherings. But I met some elders who came to the ceremonies that my uncle was running at the Prairie Island Dakota reservation. I sat down and talked with them. I learned they didn't want to be disrespectful to Native peoples or our ways. I talked about the importance of keeping things in context and not mixing things up. They understood. They said there was no structure in the Rainbow tribe to address this. They do the best they can—basically they allow different people to do what they want to do.

I started to pray about that. An understanding came to me that God is very compassionate and loving to everyone. When people come together searching for answers for themselves, like the Rainbow tribe, if they are sincere and have patience, a way will come to them that is for them. It may not be Native as we define it, but it is something that comes in a sacred manner and it will be for them. That is the power of this Creation working through all people of all races and all tribes.

It is my prayer that when all humans go through this transformation, it will help them to re-identify their relationship to the sacredness of the land, Mother Earth. When this comes, we will have peace and a clean and safe future for our future generations.

Reading Set Number 10: Peasant Resistance

Problem: What is the role of small farmers in today's world?

Exercise: Keep a food diary for a day and then try to discover how much of your diet was produced by small farmers and how much by large, agribusiness concerns. You may have to do some searching on the Internet.

Today's members of industrial societies sit down to a meal whose parts have traveled an average of 1500 miles. Regardless of climate, fresh fruit and vegetables are available year around. Yet rarely do people consider where their food came from and who produced it. A century ago, half of all Americans were food producers. Today it is now less than 2%. Yet all over the world, billions of people still depend on what they grow in order to survive. However, as in the United States over the past century, their number is shrinking.

One of the major problems for small farmers in Third World countries is free trade. As the article in this set on the problems of Mexican farmers indicates, free trade has allowed large-scale U.S. factory farms to export their produce to poor countries at prices well below what the small farmer can produce and sell it for.

Furthermore, the U.S. has not kept its promises to allow the import of produce, such as sugar, into the U.S. The result is the impoverishment of small farmers and growing dependence on U.S. agricultural imports.

The second article by Katherine Ainger details how multinational corporations, with the help of free trade agreements, are making it impossible for small farmers to survive in either the non-industrial or industrial countries. She also describes the efforts of organizations of peasants and small farmers to protect their livelihood The problem, of course, is that if all the small farmers stop growing their own food, then who will feed them?

Study Questions 10

1. Why has NAFTA created a problem for Mexican farmers?

2. Why can't Mexican sugar growers sell their product in the United States?

3. Why do farmers in Europe and North America receive less of the money spent by food consumers than they did 50 years ago?

4. What are some of the goals of Via Campesina?

Reading Number 1: Farm Unrest Roils Mexico, Challenging New President by GINGER THOMPSON (NY Times, July 22, 2001)

AMATLAN, Mexico The fields are green with new sugar cane, but the peasant farmers feel that their way of life is withering away.

By the tens of thousands, peasants in Mexico are abandoning the small plots they considered their birthright.

In recent weeks, thousands of other peasants have taken their struggles to the streets, even to the nation's capital, pushing parts of the agricultural industry to the brink of civil unrest.

The small farmers, typically with plots of just a few acres, are being battered by a combination of forces, from the explosion of free trade under NAFTA to plummeting market prices and cuts in government support. Rice, corn and coffee farmers are all being hurt.

Just as American growers from California to Mississippi to Florida complain that the free trade accord with the United States has forced hundreds of them out of business, Mexico's farmers feel similarly overwhelmed. They complain that they, too, are drowning in a flood of imports, and that the agreement has not given them the access to American markets they were promised.

For President Vicente Fox, who inherited a crisis rooted in decades of

paternalism and corruption in the long-ruling Institutional Revolutionary

Party, reforming the agricultural industry and finding alternative

employment for millions of subsistence farmers at a time of widespread

resentment may prove his most important domestic challenge.

This month, 5,000 sugar cane farmers converged on the capital and blocked access to government offices, demanding $420 million from the nation's 60 sugar mills. The protests became furious after government officials announced that they would investigate charges of corruption against one of the nation's most powerful milling companies.

Tens of thousands of other farmers have held their own protests, forcing one state governor to declare an emergency. Several other governors admit to being worried that the protests could cause smoldering uprisings to ignite.

"The entire Mexican countryside is a disaster," said Carmelo Balderas, hacking with a hoe at weeds around the young sugar plants in his two-acre field near the San Miguelito mill in Amatlan in the state of Veracruz.

"There is almost no place left in the country where a small farmer can make a good living."

"And the problem for Mexico," he added, "is that when farmers stop eating, everyone stops eating."

Mr. Balderas said two of his four sons had migrated to the United States in recent years. Asked why, he pointed in the direction of the San Miguelito sugar mill, slouched on a hillside overlooking the village. The mill's owners still owed Mr. Balderas $3,000 for sugar cane he produced last season. His sons, like many other young men in the village, had tired of relying on declining and unreliable incomes.

A wry smile spread across Mr. Balderas' sun-bronzed face, and he compared the crumbling mill to an Aztec pyramid. Soon, he said, "the mill will be the only evidence that we ever existed."

Some of the most intense protests began early this month in the northeastern state of Sinaloa. Corn farmers blocked access to gas depots to demand that the government impose higher tariffs on corn imported from the United States. In all, there are 3.5 million corn growers across the country, and they are uniformly overwhelmed by a 45 percent drop in corn prices over three years.

Farmers in Sinaloa contend that importing corn from the United States has left them with 2.4 million tons of unsold corn. Imports have increased by 14 percent a year or more since the North American Free Trade Agreement took effect in 1994. That landmark agreement encompasses Mexico, the United States and Canada.

After two days of protests, the governor of Sinaloa, Juan S. Millan, declared a state of emergency when panicked motorists began hoarding gasoline and the state's most important businesses, particularly hotels in the resort city of Mazatlan, were forced to close or greatly reduce their services.

A few days later, in the state of Campeche, rice farmers took control of two cereal plants to demand that the government renegotiate $4 million in loans. And in mid-July, the governors of nine coffee-producing states agreed to press the national government to create an emergency fund to help compensate coffee farmers devastated by declining prices.

The governors, including those from Veracruz, Oaxaca and Nayarit, pointed out that the crises in their states had generated new waves of migrants to the United States. And using the experience of his own state as a warning, the governor of Chiapas, Pablo Salazar, said the areas most affected were those most prone to armed uprisings.

[On July 20, farmers in the border state of Chihuahua gathered at a customs station and turned back grain shipments from the United States. A leader at the protest, part of a national peasant farmer movement called El Barzsn, told Mexican reporters that the demonstrations would last until the government undertook new initiatives to help small farmers.]

Mexico's sugar industry offers a window on problems as complex and entangled as the web of shafts and conveyer belts in the sugar mill here.

In the decades after the 1910 Mexican revolution, the government distributed millions of small plots of land more than half the nation's territory to peasants as a way of fostering peace in the poorest regions. Over time, those plots have become even smaller as they have been divided and handed down to children and grandchildren. Today each of the nation's sugar mills is supplied by thousands of cane growers each with an average of just four acres of sugar cane.

The San Miguelito refinery has contracts with 4,500 growers, said Ramsn Martmnez Amaya, the refinery's controller. Unions, once a part of the Institutional Revolutionary Party's authoritarian political machine, determine the size of the refinery's bloated work force. At the start of the harvest last December, tens of thousands of mill workers called a national strike to demand a 25 percent wage increase and improved retirement benefits.

And under the law governing the sugar industry, the government sets the prices that mills pay cane farmers and requires that the mills make most of those payments before the end of the harvest in May.

Even after it sold the mills to private investors in the late 1980's, the Institutional Revolutionary Party government continued to set prices and to force mills to adhere to union demands.

San Miguelito, like many of the nation's sugar mills, is in serious disrepair. There is a field of new parts and machinery out back, but Mr. Martmnez said there was no money for installation. "In global terms," he said, "this plant is way behind modern times."

Rodolfo Perdomo Bueno, who operates a mill company called Grupo Perno, said that despite their outdated machinery, Mexico's refineries had increased sugar production during the last seven years in anticipation of the opening of United States sugar markets under NAFTA.

According to the Mexican government, by last October NAFTA should have let mills export all their excess sugar, an estimated 500,000 tons, to the United States. But a so-called "side letter," added to the agreement by the United States but not recognized by Mexico, limits exports to the United States to 116,000 tons to protect the American sugar industry.

Meanwhile, Mr. Perdomo said, the Mexican sugar market is steadily shrinking because of increasing imports of less costly high fructose corn syrup from the United States. The syrup is preferred by Mexico's important soft drink industry.

"We were betrayed," Mr. Perdomo said. "We are being forced to sell our sugar wherever we can, at whatever price, so that we don't drown in it."

In Amatlan, sugar farmers wait for what they are owed. Many said the San Miguelito mill owed them $1,500 to $3,000 for the season. It was all the money many would earn this year.

For Mr. Fox, lifting Mexico's rural communities, which make up about 28 percent of the population, out of poverty is a daunting challenge. The son of ranchers, he has promised to help subsistence farmers find new markets, organize themselves into farming cooperatives, and find financing to modernize operations. In recent weeks, his administration has negotiated agreements with corn farmers in Sinaloa and cane growers in Veracruz that have essentially secured the payments they are owed.

But Mr. Fox, a former corporate executive, is also committed to the more Darwinesque principles of free trade. And members of his administration have said that in Mr. Fox's modern-day revolution, small farmers are facing a harsh reality: not all will survive.

In an interview, Secretary of Agriculture Javier Usabiaga said the government could not afford the paternalistic programs that kept small farms going in the past. Rather than charity, Mr. Usabiaga said, the Fox administration wants to change the way the industry is organized.

"We have to change an entire culture," he said. "A small farmer, no matter how productive, is not going to be able to make enough money to survive. That farmer is going to have to start transforming his crops to milk, meat or anything else.

"In essence, he is going to have to find another job," Mr. Usabiaga said. "He is going to have to become a part-time farmer."

But at least one family in Amatlan has decided to break with generations of tradition. Tired of depending on mill officials to pay for the sugar cane they produced, Mari Cruz Hernandez and her husband, Daniel Beristain, decided to grow fruit and flowers on the acre they inherited from her mother. On a recent day, they began planting lychee plants on half an acre. On the other half they plan to plant gladiolas.

The gladiolas, Ms. Cruz hopes, will bloom every four months and support her, her husband and her elderly mother for the three years that it will take the fruit plants to begin to yield.

"I got tired of working all year, and then in the end the mill wouldn't pay," she said. "They made us into working beggars. And so we decided, no more."

Many young men in the village, she said, seemed to be making similar decisions. Ms. Cruz pointed to a passing train on tracks above her fields. It was the morning train heading south, she said, toward Guatemala.

The northbound train, she said, passes each evening. Hundreds of Central Americans bound for the United States hang from the cars. And increasingly, she said, young men from the village have begun hopping on board.

Going north has crossed her mind, Ms. Cruz, 28, acknowledged. She compared the migrants to pioneers, and said that each time the migrant train passed, she whispered a prayer for God's protection. But her goals are still centered on home.

Asked about the risks of abandoning a crop that supported her family over three generations, Ms. Cruz said she considered herself a different kind of pioneer. "Sometimes you have to risk everything if you are going to get ahead," she said. "If the migrants risk everything to leave, then we can take risks to stay."

Reading Number 2: The New Peasant's Revolt by Katherine Ainger (New Internationalist Magazine, #353, January-February 2003)

Everything in a supermarket has a story to tell, if only we could find it out. The produce defies seasons, geography, wars, distance, nature. It is winter outside, but inside the supermarket golden-shell pineapples from Ctte d'Ivoire, still small and green, bathe in humming halogen light. There is civil unrest in the Ctte d'Ivoire, but it does not seem to have disrupted the flow of tropical fruit to the cold North. Next to them are strange, knobbly bits of ginger dug from Chinese soil. Gala apples from France, bagged up and reduced to half price. Avocados from Israel and Chile. Pale tomatoes from the Canary Islands, where it is always warm, but the fruit must be picked green. 'Ready-to-go' meals fill the chiller cabinets. Here, wrapped in plastic, are small clusters of perfect baby corn and mange tout from plantations in Kenya. Here is cod, pulled up by trawler from the over-fished, churning cold sea of the northeast Atlantic.

Though we can't hear their stories, what we choose to put in our supermarket baskets writes its own language upon our bodies and our moods, our families, our economies, our landscapes. It can mean life or death in some distant country whose name we can only vaguely discern printed on the packaging. We are, all of us, affected by trends in the global economy, in the most intimate and fundamental way possible - through our food.

Only rarely do these connections become visible, when the people who produce the food remind us of them. Those who work the countryside are a potent source of cultural identity, whether it's the campesinos of Mexico, the gauchos of Argentina, the paysannes of France, Australian conkies, or the flat-capped Yorkshire farmer. Their images are used to market food to us, because we associate them with rural life, nature and rude good health. But the real people who produce our food are losing their livelihoods and leaving the land.

Over the past two years British dairy farmers, in their grief and anger over plummeting prices, have blockaded supermarkets up and down the country, spilled their milk, boycotted suppliers.

Why blockade the supermarkets? The average price British farmers receive for their milk is the lowest for 30 years. The bargaining power of the supermarkets is so great that prices for farmers are going ever downwards. In 2000, supermarket giant Tesco introduced international 'reverse' auctions for its suppliers all over the world. They were asked to bid against each other until Tesco got the lowest price.

Supermarkets blame the consumer for wanting 'cheap food' -yet 50 years ago farmers in Europe and North America received between 45 and 60 per cent of the money that consumers spent on food. Today that proportion has dropped to just 7 per cent in Britain and 3.5 per cent in the US.

Even that ultimate symbol of rugged individualism, the cowboy, is an endangered species. Most of the ranchers of the Great Plains of Nebraska are permanently broke, mortgaging or selling off their land and cattle to survive. The cowboy is riding into the final sunset as the Great Plains become steadily depopulated.

The details are specific to each country but the broad trends are international: the crisis in farming is global.

The six founding countries of Europe's Common Agricultural Policy had 22 million farmers in 1957; today that number has fallen to 7 million. Just 20 per cent of the European Union's wealthiest and largest farmers get 80 per cent of EU subsidies. Canada lost three-quarters of its farmers between 1941 and 1996 and the decline continues. In 1935 there were 6.8 million working farmers in the US; today the number is under 1.9 million - less than the total US prison population.

Suicide is now the leading cause of death among US farmers, occurring at a rate three times higher than in the general population. In Britain farmers are taking their own lives at a rate of one a week.

In poorer countries the situation is even worse. Half of the world's people still make their living from the land - and it is they who feed the majority of the world's poorest people. In South Asia and sub-Saharan Africa more than 70 per cent of the population makes a living from the land. Agriculture counts, on average, for half of total economic activity.

In the Philippines the number of farm households in the corn-producing region of Mindanao is set to fall by half. Between 1985 and 1995 the number of people employed in agriculture in Brazil fell from 23 million to 18 million. In China an estimated 400 million farmers are in danger of losing their livelihoods entirely. Everywhere small-scale farmers are being 'disappeared'.

All eaten up

Why is this happening? Somebody, somewhere, must be benefiting. The answer is not hard to discover. It lies not in the soil, but inside the corporations which have become known collectively as 'agribusiness'. They traverse the planet buying at the lowest possible price, putting every farmer in direct competition with every other farmer. While the price of crops has been pushed down - often even below the cost of production - the prices of inputs such as seed, fertilizers and pesticides have gone up.

Control of the 'food-chain' is being concentrated in ever-fewer hands. According to Bill Hefferman, rural sociologist at the University of Missouri, in some cases there is 'seamless and fully integrated control of the food system from gene to supermarket shelf'. When the two giant corporations Monsanto and Cargill went into partnership they controlled seed, fertilizer, pesticides, farm finance, grain collection, grain processing, livestock-feed processing, livestock production and slaughtering, as well as several processed-food brands. This system, developed in the US, is being exported to other countries in the name of globalization.

This level of control is one of the reasons why genetically modified (GM) seeds are of such concern. They give agribusiness yet more weapons with which to enforce total dependency on their patented seeds. Some of them require own-brand herbicides and even own-brand 'trigger' chemicals (known as 'traitor' technology) that the farmer has to apply for before the seed will germinate.

This is the secret of the disappearance of the family farmer in the North - and the peasantry in the South. To disappear them, aside from killing them, you must turn them into vulnerable workers on an assembly line, without control over their own operations, and obliged to corporations.

Agribusiness writes the rules of international trade. Cargill was largely responsible for the Agreement on Agriculture at the World Trade Organization (WTO), which liberalizes the global market in agricultural goods. Farmers, particularly in poor countries, find it impossible to compete with cheap imports. One James Enyart of Monsanto said of the WTO's 'intellectual property' agreement (known as 'TRIPs') which makes its ownership of seeds and genetic material possible worldwide: 'Industry has identified a major problem in international trade. It crafted a solution, reduced it to a concrete proposal and sold it to our own and other governments.'

Why does it matter that small, 'inefficient' producers are being eradicated by globalized, corporate agriculture?

Free-trade theory is based on the idea that countries should specialize, produce the things that they make best and buy in everything else. But, as Kevan Bundell from Christian Aid says: 'It makes little sense for poor countries or poor farmers to put themselves at more risk if they have to rely on the efficient functioning of markets which all too often fail or don't exist.'

How 'efficient' is a system of agriculture that ignores ('externalizes') the huge costs of removing chemical contamination from water or losing genetic diversity? How 'wholesome' is it to create new diseases in animals and antibiotic resistance in people? How 'cheap' is the expense of public subsidies to private agribusiness, of global transport or social breakdown in rural areas?

Prevailing free-market thinking asks why we should provide support just to keep people in a state of 'backwardness' and rural poverty. But experience shows us that when these people lose their rural livelihoods, only a few will find better jobs in the city. Many will end up in enormous and growing urban slums.

'The future for peasant incomes and employment is grim,'says Chen Xiwen, deputy director of the Chinese State Council's research center. According to Chen, in 2001 over 88 million workers migrated from rural to urban areas in China, most of them employed in 'dirty, hard, dangerous and unsafe conditions'.

The question is not whether we have any right to condemn people to the difficult life of a poor farmer - an accusation often thrown at those who oppose the global-trade regime and the food cartel that runs it. The real question is whether vulnerable farmers themselves have meaningful choices. They need an international voice for their own priorities.

Let them eat trade Nettie Webb, a Canadian farmer explains:

'The difficulty for us, as farming people, is that we are rooted in the places where we live and grow our food. The other side, the corporate world, is globally mobile.'

To put it another way, global- trade rules might be fundamentally transforming agriculture, but as one sceptic asked: 'can one envision a coalition of Belgian, Dutch, French, Italian, Uruguayan, Brazilian and New Zealand farmers marching on a GATT (WTO) meeting in Punta del Este?

And what could they demand to benefit them all, since they are all in competition with one another?

In fact Via Campesina has been marching on every WTO meeting from 1994 onwards. 'We will not be intimidated. We will not be "disappeared",' they have declared. This global alliance of small and family farmers, peasants, landless and indigenous people, women and rural laborers, has a membership of millions - the vast majority from poor countries - and they're putting an alternative agricultural paradigm on the map.

It's based on the idea of 'food sovereignty'. It is, they say, 'the RIGHT of peoples, communities and countries to define their own agricultural, labor, fishing, food and land policies which are ecologically, socially, economically and culturally appropriate to their unique circumstances.'

They believe food is a human right, not a commodity, and that their job - the production of food - is fundamental to all human existence. This attitude is summed up by a food co-op member's retort to Brazilian President Cardoso when he said that agriculture had to submit to the law of the market: 'Very well, Mr President. When Brazil no longer needs food, then you can let agriculture go bankrupt.'

The farmers of Via Campesina argue that nothing as important as food should be ruled by the WTO. They've been leading the campaign to take agriculture out of its remit entirely. This does not mean that they are 'anti-trade'. They believe in trading goods which a country cannot produce itself. Once a country has supported its own food needs and production it should be free to trade the surplus.

I spent time with Via Campesina at the 2002 World Social Forum in Porto Alegre, Brazil, where they explained their vision in more depth. I'm in the courtyard of the Convent del Capuchino. There are mango and papaya trees hung with unripe green fruit. Via Campesina delegates - people of few words - sit on benches, sip sweet coffee and contemplate.

Josi Bocquisso Jr explains the views of the National Peasants' Union in Mozambique. 'Mozambique was one of the largest cashew-nut processors in the world,' he says. 'But because of the IMF the industry was privatized and the processing plants were closed... People should concentrate on producing food for themselves, not products for export... If we produce a lot of cotton the price ends up being below the cost of production, and people are stranded with piles of cotton, but with no food and no money. In our organization we concentrate on producing food, we encourage our members first to provide for their daily needs.

Then it doesn't matter so much if they don't have money, because they are secure in food and have guaranteed the ability to feed their families.' His group is part of the expanding African contingent in Via Campesina. 'It is very strengthening to feel part of a global movement. World powers have to be fought globally.'

Via Campesina is not anti-technology. Its vision is, however, based on a model of agriculture built from the ground up, in which farmers' knowledge has a significant place. Indeed, all Via Campesina's arguments about food and farming - whether GMOs, access to land or markets - come down to one central issue: control.

Indra Lubis, part of a coalition of 13 Indonesian peasant unions with 900,000 members, explains that rejection of genetically modified seed and pesticides is about self-determination: 'With Monsanto, who have planted GM cotton in south Sulawesi, we'll have to depend on them for seed. They want to control cotton and food production. As peasants, we'll be made dependent on multinational corporations. But we are independent when we develop our own agriculture. We use our own productive system, with no chemical fertilizer or herbicides. We use local seeds and local fertilizer. In Indonesia we have so many varieties of seed. It is a deep part of our culture.'

Seventy per cent of the world's farmers are women - most of the people in this courtyard are men. Rosalva Gutierrez, from the Belize Association of Producer Organizations, tells me: 'It is always the women who take the hardest part as farmers, mothers, wives. We have many strong women but they have been abused for so many years, women's self-esteem is very low. So we give workshops and training... I'm co-ordinator of the women's project and on the international co-ordination of Via Campesina - I try to ensure that what Via Campesina says on paper about gender equality becomes reality!'

And she tells me: 'We don't see farmers as being from different countries. Farmers everywhere understand the same point.'

Via Campesina argues that food production has a unique role to play in rural livelihoods, health, ecology and culture.

Kanya Pankiti, a peasant from the south of Thailand - on her first trip out of the country - says the way her people grow food preserves the forest, the watershed and the soil. She thinks the Brazilians aren't growing enough trees. 'The way Brazilians do agriculture now will cause soil erosion,' she worries, picking and nibbling leaves she recognizes from home - it has never occurred to Brazilians to cook with them.

Kanya knows a lot about trees. She says: 'The Thai forest department doesn't believe that people can live in the forest and preserve it. The reality is, we have lived in the forest for a hundred years. It is not the villagers who are destroying the forest, but the loggers clear-cutting. When the forest is clear-cut the land becomes less fertile.' Her house is outside a new National Park zone, her land inside it, and they want to clear her out. 'When they declare a National Park,' she says, 'they sit in an air-conditioned office and look at a map.'

What does she think of the World Social Forum? She's going back to tell her village 'that they are not alone in the world, struggling for land, and we can link up with those in other countries'.

For anyone who eats, the question of who controls the food chain - farmers, or an ever-more powerful cartel of food corporations - is no less pertinent than it is for Indra, Kanya or Josi. At the very same time as consumers in the rich world are objecting more than ever to factory farming, to the use of antibiotics in livestock, to pesticide residues in food, to the loss of biodiversity and to food scares such as BSE, this very same model is being set up for replication around the world, often disguised as 'development'.

Mario Pizano, a member of the Confederacisn Campesino del Suerto in Chile, joins the conversation. 'The big companies are buying up all the land,' he complains. 'With contract farming, they tell us: "We'll buy your food only if you buy the chemicals you need from us." They give us chemicals that are forbidden in the US. Then we have to give them a section of our crop. If we can't, then they take our land.'

But he, and millions like him, refuse to become serfs on their own land. As we part, he takes off his green cap, emblazoned with the name of his organization, and gives it to me. 'This organization is part of me,' he says.

Reading Set Number 11: Antisystemic Resistance

> Problem: What are some of the factors that lead groups or individuals to use violence to address what they perceive as oppression and marginalization?
>
> How does one define violence used by groups to resist what they feel or perceive as oppression? Is it true that "one person's terrorist is another's freedom fighter"?

> Exercise: Each year in the United States, over 11,000 people are killed by guns. Yet, if the preventive measures taken by our government are any indication, more people are more afraid of "terrorists than of gun owners. What are some of the reasons for this?

The term anti-systemic movement was coined by Immanuel Wallerstein to describe attempts by groups or individuals to resist the negative aspects of the market economy. Labor movements, environmental movements, anti-colonial movements, feminist movements, and militia movements constitute examples of this form of resistance. Historically anti-systemic resistance turns violent either in response to efforts to violently subdue resistance or as a purposive strategy to achieve economic or political goals. Often violent resistance is referred to as "terrorism." But what is terrorism and is violent resistance under any circumstances illegitimate?

The following two articles address this issue. Noam Chomsky has written extensively on terrorism. His article poses the question of the difference between "their" terrorism and "our" terrorism." That is, if the U.S. is directly or indirectly responsible for violent acts that fit its own definition of terrorism, how can violent actions be condemned in the one case and celebrated in the other? Chomsky asks, for example, how was the violence sponsored or supported by the U.S. in Nicaragua or Lebanon, any different than the violence committed by Osama bin Ladan?

The second article by John Brown raises another issue crucial to the exercise of dissent: how does one define "terrorism" precisely enough to protect legitimate, democratic protest? Brown argues that current legal definitions could permit law enforcement authorities to treat labor, environmental, or any form of anti-systemic protest as terrorism.

Study Questions 11

1. Why is it difficult to differentiate legitimate collective violence from that which is illegitimate?

2. Why, according to Chomsky, did the "war against terror" declared by the United States, have little resonance?

3. Why is defining terrorism as "illegal warfare" problematical?

4. How can most state-sanctioned definitions of terrorism be used to stifle any form of political dissent?

Reading Number 1. Who are the Global Terrorists? *by Noam Chomsky*
(Reprinted from Ken Booth and Tim Dunne eds., Worlds in Collision: Terror and the Future of Global Order, Palgrave/Macmillan, UK, May 2002)

After the atrocities of 11 September, the victim declared a "war on terrorism," targeting not just the suspected perpetrators, but the country in which they were located, and others charged with terrorism worldwide. President Bush pledged to "rid the world of evildoers" and "not let evil stand," echoing Ronald Reagan's denunciation of the "evil scourge of terrorism" in 1985 -- specifically, state-supported international terrorism, which had been declared to be the core issue of US foreign policy as his administration came into office. The focal points of the first war on terror were the Middle East and Central America, where Honduras was the major base for US operations. The military component of the re-declared war is led by Donald Rumsfeld, who served as Reagan's special representative to the Middle East; the diplomatic efforts at the UN by John Negroponte, Reagan's Ambassador to Honduras. Planning is largely in the hands of other leading figures of the Reagan-Bush (I) administrations.

The condemnations of terrorism are sound, but leave some questions unanswered. The first is: What do we mean by "terrorism"? Second: What is the proper response to the crime? Whatever the answer, it must at least satisfy a moral truism: If we propose some principle that is to be applied to antagonists, then we must agree -- in fact, strenuously insist -- that the principle apply to us as well. Those who do not rise even to this minimal level of integrity plainly cannot be taken seriously when they speak of right and wrong, good and evil.

The problem of definition is held to be vexing and complex. There are, however, proposals that seem straightforward, for example, in US Army manuals, which define terrorism as "the calculated use of violence or threat of violence to attain goals that are political, religious, or ideological in nature...through intimidation, coercion, or instilling fear." That definition carries additional authority because of the timing: it was offered as the Reagan administration was intensifying its war on terrorism. The world has changed little enough so that these recent precedents should be instructive, even apart from the continuity of leadership from the first war on terrorism to its recent reincarnation.

The first war received strong endorsement. The UN General Assembly condemned international terrorism two months after Reagan's denunciation, again in much stronger and more explicit terms in 1987. Support was not unanimous, however. The 1987 resolution passed 153-2, Honduras abstaining. Explaining their negative vote, the US and Israel identified the fatal flaw: the statement that "nothing in the present resolution could in any way prejudice the right to self-determination, freedom, and independence, as derived from the Charter of the United Nations, of people forcibly deprived of that right..., particularly peoples under colonial and racist regimes and foreign occupation..." That was understood to apply to the struggle of the African National Congress against the Apartheid regime of South Africa (a US ally, while the ANC was officially labeled a "terrorist organization"); and to the Israeli military occupation, then in its 20th year, sustained by US military and diplomatic support in virtual international isolation. Presumably because of US opposition, the UN resolution against terrorism was ignored.

Reagan's 1985 condemnation referred specifically to terrorism in the Middle East, selected as the lead story of 1985 in an AP poll. But for Secretary of State George Shultz, the administration moderate, the most "alarming" manifestation of "state-sponsored terrorism," a plague spread by "depraved opponents of civilization itself" in "a return to barbarism in the modern age," was frighteningly close to home. There is "a cancer, right here in our land mass," Shultz informed Congress, threatening to conquer the hemisphere in a "revolution without borders," a interesting fabrication exposed at once but regularly reiterated with appropriate shudders.

So severe was the threat that on Law Day (1 May) 1985, the President announced an embargo "in response to the emergency situation created by the Nicaraguan Government's aggressive activities in Central America." He also declared a national emergency, renewed annually, because "the policies and actions of the Government of Nicaragua constitute an unusual and extraordinary threat to the national security and foreign policy of the United States."

"The terrorists -- and the other states that aid and abet them -- serve as grim reminders that democracy is fragile and needs to be guarded with vigilance," Shultz warned. We must "cut [the Nicaraguan cancer] out," and not by gentle means: "Negotiations are a euphemism for capitulation if the shadow of power is not cast across the bargaining table," Shultz declared, condemning those who advocate "utopian, legalistic means like outside mediation, the United Nations, and the World Court, while ignoring the power element of the equation." The US was exercising "the power element of the equation" with mercenary forces based in Honduras, under Negroponte's supervision, and successfully blocking the "utopian, legalistic means" pursued by the World Court and the Latin American Contadora nations -- as Washington continued to do until its terrorist wars were won.

Reagan's condemnation of the "evil scourge" was issued at a meeting in Washington with Israeli Prime Minister Shimon Peres, who arrived to join in the call to extirpate the evil shortly after he had sent his bombers to attack Tunis, killing 75 people with smart bombs that tore them to shreds among other atrocities recorded by the prominent Israeli journalist Amnon Kapeliouk on the scene. Washington cooperated by failing to warn its ally Tunisia that the bombers were on the way. Shultz informed Israeli Foreign Minister Yitzhak Shamir that Washington "had considerable sympathy for the Israeli action," but drew back when the Security Council unanimously denounced the bombing as an "act of armed aggression" (US abstaining).

A second candidate for most extreme act of Mid-East international terrorism in the peak year of 1985 is a car-bombing in Beirut on March 8 that killed 80 people and wounded 256. The bomb was placed outside a Mosque, timed to explode when worshippers left. "About 250 girls and women in flowing black chadors, pouring out of Friday prayers at the Imam Rida Mosque, took the brunt of the blast," Nora Boustany reported. The bomb also "burned babies in their beds," killed children "as they walked home from the mosque," and "devastated the main street of the densely populated" West Beirut suburb. The target was a Shi'ite leader accused of complicity in terrorism, but he escaped. The crime was organized by the CIA and its Saudi clients with the assistance of British intelligence.

The only other competitor for the prize is the "Iron Fist" operations that Peres directed in March in occupied Lebanon, reaching new depths of "calculated brutality and arbitrary murder," a Western diplomat familiar with the area observed, as Israel Defense Forces (IDF) shelled villages, carted off the male population, killed dozens of villagers in addition to many massacred by the IDF's paramilitary associates, shelled hospitals and took patients away for "interrogation," along with numerous other atrocities. The IDF high command described the targets as "terrorist villagers." The operations against them must continue, the military correspondent of the Jerusalem Post (Hirsh Goodman) added, because the IDF must "maintain order and security" in occupied Lebanon despite "the price the inhabitants will have to pay."

Like Israel's invasion of Lebanon 3 years earlier, leaving some 18,000 killed, these actions and others in Lebanon were not undertaken in self-defense but rather for political ends, as recognized at once in Israel. The same was true, almost entirely, of those that followed, up to Peres's murderous invasion of 1996. But all relied crucially on US military and diplomatic support. Accordingly, they too do not enter the annals of international terrorism.

In brief, there was nothing odd about the proclamations of the leading co-conspirators in Mideast international terrorism, which therefore passed without comment at the peak moment of horror at the "return to barbarism."

The well-remembered prize-winner for 1985 is the hijacking of the Achille Lauro and brutal murder of a passenger, Leon Klinghoffer, doubtless a vile terrrorist act, and surely not justified by the claim that it was in retaliation for the far worse Tunis atrocities and a pre-emptive effort to deter others. Adopting moral truisms, the same holds of our own acts of retaliation or pre-emption.

Evidently, we have to qualify the definition of "terrorism" given in official sources: the term applies only to terrorism against us, not the terrorism we carry out against _them_. The practice is conventional, even among the most extreme mass murderers: the Nazis were protecting the population from terrorist partisans directed from abroad, while the Japanese were laboring selflessly to create an "earthly paradise" as they fought off the "Chinese bandits" terrorizing the peaceful people of Manchuria and their legitimate government. Exceptions would be hard to find.

The same convention applies to the war to exterminate the Nicaraguan cancer. On Law Day 1984, President Reagan proclaimed that without law there can be only "chaos and disorder." The day before, he had announced that the US would disregard the proceedings of the International Court of Justice, which went on to condemn his administration for its "unlawful use of force," ordering it to terminate these international terrorist crimes and pay substantial reparations to Nicaragua

(June 1986). The Court decision was dismissed with contempt, as was a subsequent Security Council resolution calling on all states to observe international law (vetoed by the US) and repeated General Assembly resolutions (US and Israel opposed, in one case joined by El Salvador).

As the Court decision was announced, Congress substantially increased funding for the mercenary forces engaged in "the unlawful use of force." Shortly after, the US command directed them to attack "soft targets" -- undefended civilian targets -- and to avoid combat with the Nicaraguan army, as they could do, thanks to US control of the skies and the sophisticated communication equipment provided to the terrorist forces. The tactic was considered reasonable by prominent commentators as long as it satisfied "the test of cost-benefit analysis," an analysis of "the amount of blood and misery that will be poured in, and the likelihood that democracy will emerge at the other end" -- "democracy" as Western elites understand the term, an interpretation illustrated graphically in the region.

State Department Legal Advisor Abraham Sofaer explained why the US was entitled to reject ICJ jurisdiction. In earlier years, most members of the UN "were aligned with the United States and shared its views regarding world order." But since decolonization a "majority often opposes the United States on important international questions." Accordingly, we must "reserve to ourselves the power to determine" how we will act and which matters fall "essentially within the domestic jurisdiction of the United States, as determined by the United States" -- in this case, the terrorist acts against Nicaragua condemned by the Court and the Security Council. For similar reasons, since the 1960s the US has been far in the lead in vetoing Security Council resolutions on a wide range of issues, Britain second, France a distant third.

Washington waged its "war on terrorism" by creating an international terror network of unprecedented scale, and employing it worldwide, with lethal and long-lasting effects. In Central America, terror guided and supported by the US reached its most extreme levels in countries where the state security forces themselves were the immediate agents of international terrorism. The effects were reviewed in a 1994 conference organized by Salvadoran Jesuits, whose experiences had been particularly gruesome. The conference report takes particular note of the effects of the residual "culture of terror...in domesticating the expectations of the majority vis-a-vis alternatives different to those of the powerful," an important observation on the efficacy of state terror that generalizes broadly. In Latin America, the 11 September atrocities were harshly condemned, but commonly with the observation that they are nothing new. They may be described as "Armageddon," the research journal of the Jesuit university in Managua observed, but Nicaragua has "lived its own Armageddon in excruciating slow motion" under US assault "and is now submerged in its dismal aftermath," and others fared far worse under the vast plague of state terror that swept through the continent from the early 1960s, much of it traceable to Washington.

It is hardly surprising that Washington's call for support in its war of revenge for 11 Sept. had little resonance in Latin America. An international Gallup poll found that support for military force rather than extradition ranged from 2% (Mexico) to

11% (Venezuela and Colombia). Condemnations of the 11 Sept. terror were regularly accompanied by recollections of their own suffering, for example, the death of perhaps thousands of poor people (Western crimes, therefore unexamined) when George Bush I bombed the barrio Chorillo in Panama in December 1989 in Operation Just Cause, undertaken to kidnap a disobedient thug who was sentenced to life imprisonment in Florida for crimes mostly committed while he was on the CIA payroll.

The record continues to the present without essential change, apart from modification of pretexts and tactics. The list of leading recipients of US arms yields ample evidence, familiar to those acquainted with international human rights reports.

It therefore comes as no surprise that President Bush informed Afghans that bombing will continue until they hand over people the US suspects of terrorism (rebuffing requests for evidence and tentative offers of negotiation). Or, when new war aims were added after three weeks of bombing, that Admiral Sir Michael Boyce, chief of the British Defense Staff, warned Afghans that US-UK attacks will continue "until the people of the country themselves recognize that this is going to go on until they get the leadership changed." In other words, the US and UK will persist in "the calculated use of violence to attain goals that are political... in nature...": international terrorism in the technical sense, but excluded from the canon by the standard convention. The rationale is essentially that of the US-Israel international terrorist operations in Lebanon. Admiral Boyce is virtually repeating the words of the eminent Israeli statesman Abba Eban, as Reagan declared the first war on terrorism. Replying to Prime Minister Menachem Begin's account of atrocities in Lebanon committed under the Labor government in the style "of regimes which neither Mr. Begin nor I would dare to mention by name," Eban acknowledged the accuracy of the account, but added the standard justification: "there was a rational prospect, ultimately fulfilled, that affected populations would exert pressure for the cessation of hostilities."

These concepts are conventional, as is the resort to terrorism when deemed appropriate. Furthermore, its success is openly celebrated. The devastation caused by US terror operations in Nicaragua was described quite frankly, leaving Americans "United in Joy" at their successful outcome, the press proclaimed. The massacre of hundreds of thousands of Indonesians in 1965, mostly landless peasants, was greeted with unconstrained euphoria, along with praise for Washington for concealing its own critical role, which might have embarrassed the "Indonesian moderates" who had cleansed their society in a "staggering mass slaughter" that the CIA compared to the crimes of Stalin, Hitler, and Mao. There are many other examples. One might wonder why Osama bin Laden's disgraceful exultation over the atrocities of 11 Sept. occasioned indignant surprise. But that would be an error, based on failure to distinguish their terror, which is evil, from ours, which is noble, the operative principle throughout history.

If we keep to official definitions, it is a serious error to describe terrorism as the weapon of the weak. Like most weapons, it is wielded to far greater effect by the strong. But then it is not terror; rather, "counterterror," or "low intensity warfare," or "self-defense"; and if successful, "rational" and "pragmatic," and an occasion to be "united in joy."

Let us turn to the question of proper response to the crime, bearing in mind the governing moral truism. If, for example, Admiral Boyce's dictum is legitimate, then victims of Western state terrorism are entitled to act accordingly. That conclusion is, properly, regarded as outrageous. Therefore the principle is outrageous when applied to official enemies, even more so when we recognize that the actions were undertaken with the expectation that they would place huge numbers of people at grave risk. No knowledgeable authority seriously questioned the UN estimate that "7.5 million Afghans will need food over the winter -- 2.5 million more than on Sept. 11," a 50% increase as a result of the threat of bombing, then the actuality, with a toll that will never be investigated if history is any guide.

A different proposal, put forth by the Vatican among others, was spelled out by military historian Michael Howard: "a police operation conducted under the auspices of the United Nations...against a criminal conspiracy whose members should be hunted down and brought before an international court, where they would receive a fair trial and, if found guilty, be awarded an appropriate sentence." Though never contemplated, the proposal seems reasonable. If so, then it would be reasonable if applied to Western state terrorism, something that could also never be contemplated, though for opposite reasons.

The war in Afghanistan has commonly been described as a "just war," indeed evidently so. There have been some attempts to frame a concept of "just war" that might support the judgment. We may therefore ask how these proposals fare when evaluated in terms of the same moral truism. I have yet to see one that does not instantly collapse: application of the proposed concept to Western state terrorism would be considered unthinkable, if not despicable. For example, we might ask how the proposals would apply to the one case that is uncontroversial in the light of the judgments of the highest international authorities, Washington's war against Nicaragua; uncontroversial, that is, among those who have some commitment to international law and treaty obligations. It is an instructive experiment.

Similar questions arise in connection with other aspects of the wars on terrorism. There has been debate over whether the US-UK war in Afghanistan was authorized by ambiguous Security Council resolutions, but it is beside the point. The US surely could have obtained clear and unambiguous authorization, not for attractive reasons (consider why Russia and China eagerly joined the coalition, hardly obscure). But that course was rejected, presumably because it would suggest that there is some higher authority to which the US should defer, a condition that a state with overwhelming power is not likely to accept. There is even a name for that stance in the literature of diplomacy and international relations: establishing "credibility," a standard official justification for the resort to violence, the bombing of Serbia, to mention a recent example. The refusal to consider negotiated transfer of the suspected perpetrators presumably had the same grounds.

The moral truism applies to such matters as well. The US refuses to extradite terrorists even when their guilt has been well established. One current case involves Emmanuel Constant, the leader of the Haitian paramilitary forces that were responsible for thousands of brutal killings in the early 1990s under the military junta, which Washington officially opposed but tacitly supported, publicly undermining the OAS embargo and secretly authorizing oil shipments. Constant was sentenced in absentia by a Haitian court. The elected government has repeatedly called on the US to extradite him, again on September 30, 2001, while Taliban initiatives to negotiate transfer of bin Laden were being dismissed with contempt. Haiti's request was again ignored, probably because of concerns about what Constant might reveal about ties to the US government during the period of the terror. Do we therefore conclude that Haiti has the right to use force to compel his extradition, following as best it can Washington's model in Afghanistan? The very idea is outrageous, yielding another prima facie violation of the moral truism.

It is all too easy to add illustrations. Exceptions are rare, and the reactions they Consider Cuba, probably the main target of international terrorism since 1959, remarkable in scale and character, some of it exposed in declassified documents on Kennedy's Operation Mongoose and continuing to the late 1990s. Cold War pretexts were ritually offered as long as that was possible, but internally the story was the one commonly unearthed on inquiry. It was recounted in secret by Arthur Schlesinger, reporting the conclusions of JFK's Latin American mission to the incoming President: the Cuban threat is "the spread of the Castro idea of taking matters into one's own hands," which might stimulate the "poor and underprivileged" in other countries, who "are now demanding opportunities for a decent living" -- the "virus" or "rotten apple" effect, as it is called in high places The Cold War connection was that "the Soviet Union hovers in the wings, flourishing large development loans and presenting itself as the model for achieving modernization in a single generation."

True, these exploits of international terrorism -- which were quite serious -- are excluded by the standard convention. But suppose we keep to the official definition. In accord with the theories of "just war" and proper response, how has Cuba been entitled to react?

It is fair enough to denounce international terrorism as a plague spread by "depraved opponents of civilization itself." The commitment to "drive the evil from the world" can even be taken seriously, if it satisfies moral truisms -- not, it would seem, an entirely unreasonable thought.

Reading Number 2. Euro Law Wrongly Defines Terrorism by John Brown. (Le Monde Diplomatique, February 2002)

We are told that the world will never be the same after 11 September. This much repeated claim has been used to justify a long series of repressive laws at a national and European level. It has served to make a state of emergency look normal. The draft framework decision on terrorism that the European Commission (EC) has presented to the European Council and parliament is part and parcel of this approach. The attempt to establish a minimum definition of terrorism, and the corresponding penalties, common to all members of the European Union is a decisive step in international penal doctrine. To fully understand its importance we need to look back at how international anti-terrorist legislation has evolved.

As if guided by some awful portent, anti-terrorist legislation concentrated, until the 1990s, on aviation, the weak link in worldwide transport of goods and persons. Initially, the fight against terrorism remained within the bounds of conventional penal law, seeking to punish and prevent specific acts (hijacking, taking of hostages, bomb attacks). Terrorism as such was not even mentioned.

The word first appeared in international law in two relatively recent texts: the International Convention for the Suppression of Terrorist Bombing (New York, 15 December 1997) and the International Convention for the Suppression of the Financing of Terrorism (ICSFT, New York, 9 December 1999). Neither text provided a definition of terrorism.

Law-makers seem reluctant to define a term that nevertheless appears in the title of these conventions. Indeed, a full-blown judicial doctrine has emerged from the refusal to provide a clear definition of terrorism. As the EC explains in section 2 of its proposal, "The Convention for the Suppression of Financing Terrorism states that it is an offence to provide or collect funds, directly or indirectly, unlawfully and intentionally, with the intent to use them or knowing that they will be used to commit any act included within the scope of the previously mentioned Conventions (apart from the Convention on offences and certain other offences committed on board aircraft, which is not included). This means that, even though in most of those conventions the words 'terrorism' or 'terrorist acts' are not mentioned, they are related to terrorist offences." Are we to suppose that certain international laws, in 1960-80, were anti-terrorist without even realizing it?

Perhaps not. The aim of the early texts was to encourage international cooperation to combat certain particularly dangerous or repellent acts of violence. In a democracy, the notion of political crime does not exist. The law punishes acts, never opinions. It was consequently essential to uphold a distinction between political action and terrorism, so that the latter could be covered by conventional law.

According to Article 6 of the ICSFT, "Each State Party shall adopt such measures as may be necessary, including, where appropriate, domestic legislation, to ensure that criminal acts within the scope of this Convention are under no circumstances justifiable by considerations of a political, philosophical, ideological, racial, ethnic, religious or other similar nature." Legislation focuses on the non-political side of terrorism. By systematically ignoring the political aims of terrorist action - the only feature that distinguishes it from ordinary crime - law-makers have made it impossible to define.

In addition to the activities singled out by international conventions, the ICSFT (Article 2.1.b) condemns "Any other act intended to cause death or serious bodily injury to a civilian, or to any other person not taking an active part in the hostilities in a situation of armed conflict, when the purpose of such act, by its nature or context, is to intimidate a population, or to compel a Government or an international organization to do or to abstain from doing any act".

An illegal form of warfare

This was, in fact, the first attempt at a definition of terrorism, but it juxtaposed two contradictory conceptions of the problem. The first approach emphasized injuries to civilians and was a direct descendant of the principles established by the Nuremberg Tribunal. The second approach focused on attempts to subvert political order, much as the United Kingdom Terrorism Act 2000. It also inspired the EC's recent proposal.

The various laws and conventions categorize terrorism as a form of illegal warfare, because it attacks civilians, who, at least according to traditional rules, are supposed to remain on the sidelines of conflict, which only involves armed forces. Terrorism has consequently been placed in the same category as war crimes, under the definition established by the Nuremberg Tribunal:

"Violations of the laws or customs of war which include, but are not limited to, murder, ill-treatment or deportation to slave-labor or for any other purpose of civilian population of or in occupied territory; murder or ill-treatment of prisoners of war, of persons on the Seas, killing of hostages, plunder of public or private property, wanton destruction of cities, towns, or villages, or devastation not justified by military necessity".

This seems the most acceptable definition of terrorism, if one is required. It does not involve political considerations, but sees terrorist acts as causing severe damage to society and individuals. Yet "violations of the laws and customs of war" and attacks on civilians have been an essential part of conflicts since the beginning of the 20th century. Indeed the majority of the victims of war have been civilians. Ever since war was forbidden - by the Briand-Kellogg pact of 1928, which condemned war as a means of solving international conflicts - the enemy has been a criminal and the old "laws or customs" that protected civilians have been disregarded.

To avoid incriminating states, a specific difference that distinguishes terrorism from war crimes is required. The answer is its political end. The second part of the ICSFT recognizes that terrorism aims "to intimidate a population, or to compel a Government or an international organisation to do or to abstain from doing any act". This represents a radical change of focus. Gone are the meticulous lists and descriptions of odious crimes that completely ignore

147

underlying political aims. In comes a new category of offence, characterized by its political finality. Characteristically, the inspiration for this revolution did not come from our legislative bodies but from the police.

The notion of political finality is rooted in a police definition of terrorism that appears in the list of duties allocated to the Director of the US Federal Bureau of Investigation (FBI). "Terrorism includes the unlawful use of force and violence against persons or property to intimidate or coerce a government, the civilian population, or any segment thereof, in furtherance of political or social objectives".

Although under conventional penal law attempts to define terrorism run into obstacles rooted in democratic principles, the FBI's definition has provided recent legislation with a way out. This is apparent in both the United Kingdom's Terrorism Act 2000 and the EC's recent proposal.

The UK Terrorism Act 2000 makes some minor stylistic changes but the underlying definition is the same. Terrorism, it states, "means the use or threat of action ... designed to influence the government or to intimidate the public or a section of the public ... for the purpose of advancing a political, religious or ideological cause". The text refers to the two main aims of terrorism cited in the FBI definition: attempts to influence or exert pressure on government or the public, and the political goals of action, which may also take a religious or ideological form.

The definition used by the EC is scarcely different. It does however restrict the scope of the term to a series of acts which recall existing international legislation - murder, threats, taking of hostages, bomb attacks, etc. - but adds a whole list of other offences closer to civil disobedience or protest by unions or citizen action groups, such as occupying public places and infrastructure facilities, damage to property of symbolic importance, and "attacks through interference with an information system". It is the underlying political intent that ties all these acts together. An anti-capitalist action, using dubious but in non-violent methods, could thus be considered as terrorism.

Some might claim that it is unreasonable to draw this conclusion, but the text speaks for itself. Although it lists a series of specific acts, it fails to define them clearly. To characterize them as terrorist acts, the text invokes the notion of intention, always a suspect solution in penal law.

No punishment without law

A Latin saying sums up the limits on any legal system that seeks to protect civil liberties: Nullum crimen sine lege; nulla poena sina lege (there can be no punishment of crime without a pre-existing law). This basic principle requires that offences be defined as precisely as possible, leaving the authorities very little margin for interpretation. If a broad interpretation of a law is possible, all sorts of other activities can be treated as crimes simply by analogy. According to a popular adage, if you give an inch, people will take a mile. Much the same principle applies in law to prevent excessive use of analogy.

If, on the contrary, analogy is allowed too much leeway in courts, any act may be seen as an offence simply because there is common ground between the two. This opens the door to all forms of abuse. It is increasingly common for the police to overstep its role as an auxiliary to the legal system and meddle with judiciary or legislative matters. The EU is making rapid progress in unifying its police (Europol). In the meantime, little or nothing has been done to harmonize national legislation in member states and set up common judicial bodies to uphold individual rights. The attacks on 11 September supposedly justified an extension of police powers, which otherwise would have been seen as a threat to democracy.

In the proposed European anti-terrorist legislation, terrorist acts are defined by their goals. All terrorists claim to subvert the powers that be. By analogy, anyone "seriously altering or destroying the political, economic, or social structures of a country" and committing any one of a series of poorly defined offences, may count as a terrorist. In keeping with police thinking, the key consideration for pinning a terrorist offence on a suspect is not the act but the intention. In short, the subject comes to be seen as a dangerous individual.

Prosecuting terrorism throughout the EU, as the EC intends, may [SIC!] have a negative effect on democracy. This legislation will target individuals or groups with a perfectly legitimate desire to radically change the political, economic and social organization of one or more countries. They will not be prosecuted for anything they have actually done, but because they may have done it for ideological reasons.

Reading Set Number 12: Religious Protest

Problem: Why has religious resistance gained such prominence in the world today and does religion support or undermine civic action?

Exercise: In his book, *Culture of Disbelief*, Stephen Carter argues that our effort to banish religion from politics forces people to act as though their faith does not matter to them. Yet in other countries, religion is a major religious force. Under what conditions do you think religion should play a role in government?

Historically religion has always had a revolutionary component. Religious movements emerge generally in response to some perceived injustice or from a general dissatisfaction with the state of things. Occasionally these movements have a militant or violent component. The violence may be a response to an attempt by state authorities to suppress the movement, or as a strategy to achieve political ends. Regardless, there are few places in the world today in which religious violence of one sort or another is not part of the political landscape.

The article by Mark I. Pinsky details the extent to which religion has become a political force in the world and outlines some of the reasons people are attracted to religious movements.

In the second society Timothy Brown asks whether religion subverts or enhances civic society and traces the involvement of religion in creating a better society, an involvement, he notes, that can lead also to religious intolerance. However, globalization can, he notes overcome that, in spite of the publicity given to violent religious resistance.

Study Questions 12

1. What are some of the reasons that religion provides an attractive political vehicle to those dissatisfied with the political or economic state of things?

2. What are some of the targets of today's religious movements?

3. According to Brown, where does the idea of "civic society come from?

4. How might globalization lead to greater religious tolerance?

Reading Number 1: On A String and a Prayer: In nation after nation religion has taken on a role as the primary force for political change by *Mark I. Pinsky (The Orlando Sentinel,* December 14, 1997)

With the Cold War over and global capitalism triumphant, religion has become the engine that drives the world's political and military struggles.

Believers are on a diverse crusade to control their countries.

"There are millions of people who have politicized religion and utilized it as a powerful political and even military tool," said Marc Gopin, who teaches conflict resolution at George Mason University in Virginia.

From Poland to the Philippines to the United States, and in dozens of countries between, religion is powering political opposition ranging from electoral activism to guerrilla warfare.

So much so, in fact, that in the past 25 years religion's political dimension has begun to overshadow the spiritual. That's because faith, the essence of religious commitment, makes a formidable motivator.

"In the absence of other forms of opposition, religion is now a great repository of anybody who feels disenfranchised by modern institutions, cut off – or turned off – alienated from the so-called blessing of modern civilization and materialism," said Gopin.

Other experts agree that religious faith has effectively replaced nationalism and Marxism, the driving forces for change that have dominated this century, as an organizing principle and unifying element.

"As the economy becomes globalized and old colonial powers collapse, then the basis for the nation state is in ethnic and religious identities," said Mark Juergensmeyer, director of global and international studies at the University of California at Santa Barbara. "The rise of religion in politics is directly related to the end of the Cold War."

In the United States, the Soviet Union's collapse has left many conservatives without an external enemy.

"Religious conservatives were elevated by default," said Earl Black, a Rice University political scientist. In fact, conservative Christians have become perhaps the largest voting bloc in a Republican coalition that has elevated the Grand Old Party from its once-minority status.

Outside North America and Western Europe, the global economy has resulted in an increasing gap between rich and poor, and in corruption and instability, said Stephen Zunes of the University of San Francisco.

"People feel that something is missing in their lives. Even people who are doing well say there is something missing in their lives," Zunes said.

"`There is a need for models that try to fulfill human needs. Religion, because of its strong ethical foundation, will likely play a role in trying to find a new model."

The world's religions provide historic antecedents to frame their modern campaigns:

• Islam, which expanded through conquest in the eighth century, is again on the march in Algeria, Turkey, Egypt, Saudi Arabia, Gaza and the West Bank, Kashmir, the Philippines and Jordan.

Opposition groups there have organized under the banner of Islam to challenge established regimes through electoral drives and/or armed struggles. In Iran and Afghanistan, this has been the route to power.

• Christianity, with its history of crusades and sectarian European wars, has played a leading role in successful political movements through the Catholic Church in Poland, the Philippines and Latin America. In communism's remaining outposts – Cuba, China, North Korea and Vietnam – and in some Muslim countries, Christianity is feared as a Trojan horse of democracy.

• Buddhism's peaceful roots have not kept Tibetans from rallying around the Dalai Lama in their battle for independence.

• Hinduism, which has battled for centuries against Moguls and Muslims on the Indian subcontinent, has made the Bharatiya Janata Party a major player in Indian politics. In Punjab, Sikh clergy are at the forefront of the drive for self-determination.

• Judaism was defined by the biblical conquest of the land of Canaan, arguably one of the first recorded campaigns of ethnic cleansing. Now, in Israel, Orthodox Jews have made common cause with West Bank settlers to bring the conservative Likud coalition to power, hoping to preserve Orthodox dominance over other branches of Judaism.

Historical roots notwithstanding, these political manifestations of religion represent a significant break with the more recent past.

Consider the past century's wars and upheavals: the Spanish-American War, the Boer War in South Africa, the Russo-Japanese War, World War I, the Russian Revolutions, World War II, the Chinese Revolution, the Cold War, Korea, the Vietnam War and the Third World's anti-colonial struggles.

While most, if not all, of these conflicts had underlying economic causes, nationalism and then Marxism powered them. Religion was hardly a factor.

Why does religion work so well today as a vehicle of opposition, resistance, insurgency and subversion?

"Religion is a commitment to God, and usually a commitment to some specific worship of God," said the Rev. Mitchell Pacwa of the University of Dallas. "One's meaning for life is more important than life itself. Secular society can't offer anything like that."

Religion provides many of the key elements of successful political struggle: discipline, inspiration, cohesion and organizational structure.

Sometimes, it also can offer the cover of legitimacy. But these movements are not all "fundamentalist."

In the Third World, political movements based on religion should be viewed as an "assertion of self-identity," said McGill University's Arvind Sharma, Birks professor of comparative religion.

In assessing religion's political role, Sharma said, "we must distinguish between orthodoxy and fundamentalism. Orthodoxy is a response to a religion's loss of piety, whereas fundamentalism is a religion's response to a loss of power."

Having made the distinction, Sharma added that "it can happen sometime that the two are connected."

In a classic 1953 movie, The Wild One, a nihilistic motorcycle gang leader is asked by a waitress, "What are you rebelling against?" Marlon Brando replies: "What've ya got?"

Religious people are asking the same question, although theirs is a wide-ranging rebellion of a very different stripe.

They tend to oppose whatever ideology, ethos or ruling governmental system they confront. Religion's contemporary targets include communism, socialism, secularism, pluralism, dictatorship, decadence, authoritarianism, modernism and feminism.

Although religious terrorism gets the most headlines, as in Egypt, Algeria and Israel, some groups take up arms only after their peaceful efforts are thwarted in some way, said Zunes of the University of San Francisco.

Electoral activism may actually represent religion's greatest hope for political influence.

The rise of Turkey's Islamist Welfare Party is "an excellent example of how dissatisfaction with the existing secular order can be turned into support for a religious party," said Bahman Baktiari, professor of political science at the University of Maine.

"People have come to religion for basic social, political and economic needs that the state has failed to provide them. The secular parties do not provide the unity that people want in a party."

**Reading Number 2: Does religion promote—or subvert—civil society?
By Timothy A. Brown (Civnet's Journal for Civic Society. january–february
1999 • vol 3. no. 1)**

On the face of it, religion seems to be posing an ever-increasing threat to the
proliferation of civil society. Even in countries where religion is not perhaps the
most important aspect of a social situation it is frequently a major factor or one
that fuels greater division between peoples.

• In the Balkans, for instance, the people of Kosovo, mainly ethnic Albanian
Muslims, desire independence from a predominantly Christian Serbia because of
years of brutal treatment.

• In India, the government recently proposed that the study of Hindu sacred texts
be compulsory for its students. The government's proposal advocated that school
curriculums be "Indianized, nationalized, and spiritualized." Since the Bharatiya
Janata Party has come to dominate Indian politics, a number of other such
measures have been forwarded by the government in its agenda of
Hindutva—an attempt at defining the Indian nation by its dominant religious
tradition, Hinduism. A number of groups and individuals, both religious and
secular, have expressed outrage at such a proposal considering the great
diversity of religions in the Indian sub-continent.

• In the Middle East, both Muslim and Jewish fundamentalist groups have played
major roles in sabotaging the peace process. Hamas, the most well-known
radical Muslim group, has defined its activities as a defense of Islam (what is
called *jihad* in the tradition). A number of fundamentalist Jewish groups also
consider their defense of Israel an undertaking sanctioned by God.

• In Afghanistan, the Muslim Taliban is more rigorously enforcing *shariah*, or
Muslim law.

• In Japan, radical religious groups have carried out a series of nerve gas
attacks.

• In Indonesia, attacks against Christian and Buddhist minorities are on the
increase.

• In America, conservative and fundamentalist Protestant and Catholic Christian
groups and coalitions are exerting a tremendous amount of pressure on the
political scene.

From these cases and more, one could argue that religion is proving to be one of
the greatest obstacles in the establishment of civil societies and one of the chief
threats to already existing civil societies. This appears to be a growing attitude
among the more liberal members of the press and of activist groups. But
religion's relationship to civil society is actually quite complex. Indeed, one could

argue that our contemporary notion of civil society has grown out of a predominant religious movement. What's also important to keep in mind is that, while the media usually gives greater attention to the most extreme religious voices, the more moderate or progressive elements of traditions often go unheard. The problem is not religion, which can coexist quite nicely with civil society, but religious fundamentalism. The bad news is that globalism may have inadvertently fomented religious fundamentalism. The good news is that globalism may also be promoting religious tolerance, a key requirement to civil society.

Civil society and the religion factor The Protestant Reformation of the 16th Century brought about a huge

Shift in Christian sensibility in the West. This changed attitude continues to be felt today, even in secular settings and attitudes. The Reformation, in its various manifestations in various European contexts, radically changed the individual Christian's relationship to their God, as well as their relation to the social sphere. In one sense, a new religious orientation was brought about. Robert Bellah, one of the more insightful writers on religion and culture, characterizes this new perspective as follows: "God's will was seen not as the basis and fulfillment of a vast and complex natural order that men must largely accept as it is—the conception of medieval Christianity as of most traditional religion—but as a mandate to question and revise every human institution in the process of building a holy community." Bellah also says that this reform opened up "entirely new possibilities of human action" and that this new religious identity was characterized by an "inner-worldly asceticism" and a "this-worldly activism."

The ideal, especially in its English, Scottish, and American form, was the formation of a "priesthood of believers" or a "community of saints." Each member of this "priesthood" was considered a free and equal moral agent responsible for carrying out and upholding God's will and reason. The sacredness of the individual in this schema was guaranteed by the equal access of all in the community to divine grace and revelation. Since each member of the religious community had this immediate and personal access to God there was no longer the need for mediation between the mundane and the divine realm or between the individual and the will of God.

This revisioning of the relationship between the individual and the divine had other repercussions. The lack of a need for mediation in this relationship was a direct protest against the institution of the Catholic Church. It was a challenge to the authority of both the priestly class and to the Pope as primary mediator between the human and divine realms. It also challenged the notion of a spiritually elite group as it was embodied in the monastic system. Authority and morality were no longer to be dictated by spiritual elites (priests and monks) but internalized in each individual. The growing availability of Biblical translations and the rise in literacy (especially in a developing middleclass) allowed for a direct and unmediated engagement with the Christian scriptures as sole authority and statement of the law. The individual became sole arbiter and interpreter of divine will.

The rejection of authority and hierarchy (and, in fact, all forms of mediation) that was at the heart of the Reformation has had a lasting impact on the West in both the religious and secular realms. Indeed, many of the fundamental ideas of a civil society can be traced to the Reformation, especially the freedom granted to the individual and one's reformist responsibility in relation to the world.

The next major stage in the development of the idea of civil society took place during the Enlightenment movements in Europe and eventually America. In those movements, the will of God was equated with the faculty of reason. Reason, as the highest of all human faculties, finds its support or grounding in the will of God. Bellah refers to this as the individual's "mandate to question and revise." Out of this enlightened sensibility also comes pragmatic and reasonable politics that by extension also have their base in God's will. This is why Adam Seligman, another important writer on the history of civil society, says that the traditional notion of civil society was based on both "reason and revelation." This transcendent or divine realm, which grounds reason, also establishes solidarity among its adherents. It creates shared values and a shared purpose, namely, the establishment of a "holy community."

Between the Reformation and the Enlightenment we have established most of the framework for what will become known as civil society. For example, two of the most important formulators of the traditional notion of civil society, John Locke and Thomas Jefferson, will each come out of these Protestant and Enlightenment traditions. The "self-evident" truths and "inalienable" rights and freedoms of individuals "guaranteed by God" that are at the core of the American Declaration of Independence largely reflect this twin legacy of the Reformation and the Enlightenment. Of course, the divine that sanctioned these rights was still understood in predominantly Christian terms. Religious freedom early on implied essentially the right to practice Christianity in its various forms. It would take time before religious freedom would be more fully realized and truly inclusive.

It is not a great leap from the early notion of civil society to our contemporary sense of such a society. Eventually, these fundamental human rights and freedoms are more and more detached from their divine sanction and become, in modern thought, self-sufficient. Today, one can hear faint echoes of the Reformation in contemporary discussions and practices of civil society. In the defense of individual rights and freedoms, in the activist role of individuals and groups, and in the general desire to create communities that more fully protect and reflect the fundamental rights of human beings, one can, in particular sense, this deep legacy of religious reform.

Unfortunately, the more liberal aspects within religious traditions—those that could favorably contribute to the establishment of more civil societies—have often been overshadowed by tendencies that run counter to civil society. For example, although the Protestant Reformation was so important in the development of civil society, that same Christian tradition has created some of the most intolerant voices on the American scene. In one sense, though, this position is partly in keeping with the traditional notion of civil society, where "religion" was still understood in predominantly Christian terms. In another sense, this tendency toward intolerance and fundamentalism is possible within any religious tradition.

For instance, the theologian Paul Tillich has defined religion as that meaningful structure through which human beings relate to their ultimate concern. Since this is an "ultimate" concern, writes Tillich, it is taken as "unconditionally serious and shows a willingness to sacrifice any finite concern that is in conflict with it." With the rising tide of fundamentalism today, we see exactly this seriousness and willingness to push to extremes in both words and acts. Again, due to the absolute and fundamental importance that religion plays in the majority of people's lives, and due to the strong sense of personal and collective identity and the worldview that it offers, this fundamentalizing tendency is somewhat inevitable. Religions are, of course, notorious for their claims of unique and exclusive access to the truth. And, as soon as such claims are made, other religious traditions—with their own unique claims to truth—will be considered a threat.

With the advent of globalism and the heightened sense of diversity that comes with it, it appears that this threat has become even more acute. Fundamentalism has partly grown out of the anxiety that may come about in the face of such diverse claims to truth. Unfortunately, it is often times the most threatened and anxious voices that are the loudest. The media has also overly emphasized these voices in its rare attempts at covering religion. In the media, religion has become nearly synonymous with fundamentalism.

Fortunately, there are other possibilities. If globalism has in part created reactionary voices within nearly every religious tradition, it has also created a host of voices that desire to overcome these fundamentalizing tendencies. Most of these voices have set aside exclusive claims of truth and have chosen instead to emphasize those aspects of their traditions that promote more civil societies. Here, the reality of diversity is being embraced. Also, instead of mere tolerance, reverence and understanding of other religious traditions is being taught.

To take one example: Over the past two summers religious people from very different religious traditions have been convening in Jerusalem to participate in what they call an "Experiment in Interreligious Dialogue." Jerusalem, of course, is a perfect place for such an experiment, being a holy city to Jews, Muslims, and Christians. It is also important in that it has seen in its history how religious intolerance can destroy communities.

The experiment was held at the Elijah School for the Study of the Wisdom of World Religions, a school that has brought together a consortium of 13 Jewish, Muslim, and Christian institutions. Elijah's director, Alon Goshen-Gottstein, says that "interfaith dialogue forms the backbone of the school," and that Elijah provides "one of the few places in Israel where the coexistence of Orthodox, Conservative, and Reform Jews is more than simply tolerated."

This past summer's interreligious dialogue was funded by UNESCO's "Roads of Faith" project and brought together a faculty of committed practitioners representing Christianity, Islam, Hinduism, Judaism, and a specialist in Egyptian religion. Also in attendance were a group of international and local students, as well as an array of guests and speakers from local religious groups. The group chose for its topic "Representing God," and in a short time created a community whose success can be "characterized by mutual listening, respect, and collective growth." Goshen-Gottstein and the other participants hope that their experiment "can serve as a model for understanding between religious communities, both in Israel and outside it."

Clearly, the key to tolerance—to civil society—is education. One could even argue that the teaching of the diversity of world religious traditions with both reverence and objectivity is one of the most important undertakings in the promotion of civil societies. As a professor of religious studies in a very religiously diverse New York City classroom, I have seen the tremendous impact this can have on students. I am constantly reminded of how little is known about religion. But, I have also discovered that the old cliche is true: a little knowledge goes a long way—both with students who are strongly committed to particular religious traditions and with students who never really took religion seriously. In both cases, not only tolerance, but also respect, understanding, and reverence are heightened; and this is absolutely imperative in today's global religious climate.

Reading Set Thirteen: The Citizen-Activist

Problem: How is it possible to affect meaningful changes in the world when democratic prerogatives are in decline?

Exercise: What issues would prompt you to actively demonstrate?

Virtually all social research indicates that civic participation and social association are in decline. Yet these are the foundations of any democratic society. If people are less involved in their communities and less involved with each other, then others (e.g. the government, the "managers," the "bureaucrats") are left to make the decisions that affect their lives. Furthermore, who is to define what the problems are that need fixing?

In the first article, Jonathan Rowe claims that economics has served to define our priorities in ways that hinder rather than help us. Economic growth, he says, is an unquestioned good, regardless of whether or not it helps or hurts us. Unless there is a questioning of the dogma of growth, there is little that can be done to solve our problems.

In the second article Robert Putnam describes some of the research on social capital that he pioneered, focusing on a study done in Italy on civic participation. Social capital, he says, consists of features of social organization that facilitate trust and cooperation, qualities necessary for persons to band together to address social problems. In other words, civic engagement is the best predictor of good government and ability to affect meaningful social progress.

Study Questions 13

1. Why according to Jonathan Rowe, is the Gross Domestic Product (GDP) a poor predictor of the health of a society?

2. What does Rowe mean by "compulsory consumption"?

3. What, according to Robert Putnam, is the best predictor of successful government?

4. What is meant by the term "network capitalism" and how does it relate to economic growth?

Reading Number 1: The Growth Consensus Unravels by Jonathan Rowe (Dollars and Sense: The Magazine of Economic Justice: Issue #224, July-August 1999)

Economics has been called the dismal science, but
beneath its gray exterior is a system of belief worthy of Pollyanna.

Yes, economists manage to see a dark cloud in every silver lining. Downturn
follows uptick, and inflation rears its ugly head. But there's a story within that
story — a gauzy romance, a lyric ode to Stuff. It's built into the language. A thing
produced is called a "good," for example, no questions asked. The word is more
than just a term of art. It suggests the automatic benediction which economics
bestows upon commodities of any kind.

By the same token, an activity for sale is called a "service." In conventional
economics there are no "dis-services," no actions that might be better left
undone. The bank that gouges you with ATM fees, the lawyer who runs up the
bill — such things are "services" so long as someone pays. If a friend or neighbor
fixes your plumbing for free, it's not a "service" and so it doesn't count.

The sum total of these products and activities is called the Gross Domestic
Product, or GDP. If the GDP is greater this year than last, then the result is called
"growth." There is no bad GDP and no bad growth; economics does not even
have a word for such a thing. It does have a word for less growth. In such a case,
economists say growth is "sluggish" and the economy is in "recession." No
matter what is growing — more payments to doctors because of worsening
health, more toxic cleanup — so long as there is more of it, then the economic
mind declares it good.

This purports to be "objective science." In reality it is a rhetorical construct with
the value judgments built in, and this rhetoric has been the basis of economic
debate in the United States for the last half century at least. True, people have
disagreed over how best to promote a rising GDP. Liberals generally wanted to
use government more, conservatives less. But regarding the beneficence of a
rising GDP, there has been little debate at all.

If anything, the Left traditionally has believed in growth with even greater fervor
than the Right. It was John Maynard Keynes, after all, who devised the growth-
boosting mechanisms of macroeconomic policy to combat the Depression of the
1930s; it was Keynesians who embraced these strategies after the War and
turned the GDP into a totem. There's no point in seeking a bigger pie to
redistribute to the poor, if you don't believe the expanding pie is desirable in the
first place.

Today, however, the growth consensus is starting to unravel across the political
spectrum and in ways that are both obvious and subtle. The issue is no longer
just the impact of growth upon the environment — the toxic impacts of industry
and the like. It now goes deeper, to what growth actually consists of and what it

means in people's lives. The things economists call "goods" and "services" increasingly don't strike people as such. There is a growing disconnect between the way people experience growth and the way the policy establishment talks about it, and this gap is becoming an unspoken subtext to much of American political life.

The group most commonly associated with an antigrowth stance is environmentalists, of course. To be sure, one faction, the environmental economists, is trying to put green new wine into the old bottles of economic thought. If we would just make people pay the "true" cost of, say, the gasoline they burn, through the tax system for example, then the market would do the rest. We'd have benign, less-polluting growth, they say, perhaps even more than now. But the core of the environmental movement remains deeply suspicious of the growth ethos, and probably would be even if the environmental impacts somehow could be lessened.

In the middle are suburbanites who applaud growth in the abstract, but oppose the particular manifestations they see around them — the traffic, sprawl and crowded schools. On the Right, meanwhile, an anti-growth politics is arising practically unnoticed. When social conservatives denounce gambling, pornography, or sex and violence in the media, they are talking about specific instances of the growth that their political leaders rhapsodize on other days.

Environmentalists have been like social conservatives in one key respect. They have been moralistic regarding growth, often scolding people for enjoying themselves at the expense of future generations and the earth. Their concern is valid, up to a point — the consumer culture does promote the time horizon of a five year old. But politically it is not the most promising line of attack, and conceptually it concedes too much ground. To moralize about consumption as they do is to accept the conventional premise that it really is something chosen — an enjoyable form of self-indulgence that has unfortunate consequences for the earth.

That's "consumption" in the common parlance — the sport utility vehicle loading up at Wal-Mart, the stuff piling up in the basement and garage. But increasingly that's not what people actually experience, nor is it what the term really means. In economics, consumption means everything people spend money on, pleasurable or not. Wal-Mart is just one dimension of a much larger and increasingly unpleasant whole. The lawyers' fees for the house settlement or divorce; the repair work on the car after it was rear-ended; the cancer treatments for the uncle who was a three-pack-a-day smoker; the stress medications and weight loss regimens — all these and more are "consumption." They all go into the GDP.

Cancer treatments and lawyer's fees are not what come to mind when environmentalists lament the nation's excess consumption, or for that matter when economists applaud America's "consumers" for keeping the world economy afloat. Yet increasingly such things are what consumption actually consists of in the economy today. More and more, it consists not of pleasurable

161

things that people choose, but rather of things that most people would gladly do without.

Much consumption today is addictive, for example. Millions of Americans are engaged in a grim daily struggle with themselves to do less of it. They want to eat less, drink less, smoke less, gamble less, talk less on the telephone — do less buying, period. Yet economic reasoning declares as growth and progress, that which people themselves regard as a tyrannical affliction.

Economists resist this reality of a divided self, because it would complicate their models beyond repair. They cling instead to an 18th century model of human psychology — the "rational" and self-interested man — which assumes those complexities away. As David McClelland, the Harvard psychologist, once put it, economists "haven't even discovered Freud, let alone Abraham Maslow." (They also haven't discovered the Apostle Paul, who lamented that "the good that I would I do not, but the evil that I would not that I do.")

Then too there's the mounting expenditure that sellers foist upon people through machination and deceit. People don't choose to pay for the corrupt campaign finance system or for bloated executive pay packages. The cost of these is hidden in the prices that we pay at the store. As I write this, the *Washington Post* is reporting that Microsoft has hired Ralph Reed, former head of the Christian Coalition, and Grover Norquist, a right-wing polemicist, as lobbyists in Washington. When I bought this computer with Windows 95, Bill Gates never asked me whether I wanted to help support a bunch of Beltway operators like these.

This is compulsory consumption, not choice, and the economy is rife with it today. People don't choose to pay some $40 billion a year in telemarketing fraud. They don't choose to pay 32% more for prescription drugs than do people in Canada. ("Free trade" means that corporations are free to buy their labor and materials in other countries, but ordinary Americans aren't equally free to do their shopping there.) For that matter, people don't choose to spend $25 and up for inkjet printer cartridges. The manufacturers design the printers to make money on the cartridges because, as the *Wall Street Journal* put it, that's "where the big profit margins are."

Yet another category of consumption that most people would gladly do without arises from the need to deal with the offshoots and implications of growth. Bottled water has become a multibillion dollar business in the United States because people don't trust what comes from the tap. There's a growing market for sound insulation and double-pane windows because the economy produces so much noise. A wide array of physical and social stresses arise from the activities that get lumped into the euphemistic term "growth."

The economy in such cases doesn't solve problems so much as create new problems that require more expenditure to solve. Food is supposed to sustain people, for example. But today the dis-economies of eating sustain the GDP instead. The food industry spends some $21 billion a year on advertising to entice people to eat food they don't need. Not coincidentally there's now a $32 billion diet and weight loss industry to help people take off the pounds that inevitably result. When that doesn't work, which is often, there is always the vacuum pump or knife. There were some 110,000 liposuctions in the United States last year; at five pounds each that's some 275 tons of flab up the tube.

It is a grueling cycle of indulgence and repentance, binge and purge. Yet each stage of this miserable experience, viewed through the pollyanic lens of economics, becomes growth and therefore good. The problem here goes far beyond the old critique of how the consumer culture cultivates feelings of inadequacy, lack and need so people will buy and buy again. Now this culture actually makes life worse, in order to sell solutions that purport to make it better.

Traffic shows this syndrome in a finely developed form. First we build sprawling suburbs so people need a car to go almost anywhere. The resulting long commutes are daily torture but help build up the GDP. Americans spend some $5 billion a year in gasoline alone while they sit in traffic and go nowhere. As the price of gas increases this growth sector will expand.

Commerce deplores a vacuum, and the exasperating hours in the car have spawned a booming subeconomy of relaxation tapes, cell phones, even special bibs. Billboards have 1-800 numbers so commuters can shop while they stew. Talk radio thrives on traffic-bound commuters, which accounts for some of the contentious, get-out-of-my-face tone. The traffic also helps sustain a $130 billion a year car wreck industry; and if Gates succeeds in getting computers into cars, that sector should get a major boost.

The health implications also are good for growth. Los Angeles, which has the worst traffic in the nation, also leads — if that's the word — in hospital admissions due to respiratory ailments. The resulting medical bills go into the GDP. And while Americans sit in traffic they aren't walking or getting exercise. More likely they are entertaining themselves orally with a glazed donut or a Big Mac, which helps explain why the portion of middle-aged Americans who are clinically obese has doubled since the 1960s.

C. Everett Koop, the former Surgeon General, estimates that some 70% of the nation's medical expenses are lifestyle induced. Yet the same lifestyle that promotes disease also produces a rising GDP. (Keynes observed that traditional virtues like thrift are bad for growth; now it appears that health is bad for growth too.) We literally are growing ourselves sick, and this puts a grim new twist on the economic doctrine of "complementary goods," which describes the way new products tend to spawn a host of others. The automobile gave rise to car wash franchises, drive-in restaurants, fuzz busters, tire dumps, and so forth. Television produced an antenna industry, VCRs, soap magazines, ad infinitum. The texts present this phenomenon as the wondrous perpetual motion machine of the market — goods beget more goods. But now the machine is producing complementary ills and collateral damages instead.

Suggestive of this new dynamic is a pesticide plant in Richmond, California, which is owned by a transnational corporation that also makes the breast cancer drug tamoxifen. Many researchers believe that pesticides, and the toxins created in the production of them, play a role in breast cancer. "It's a pretty good deal," a local physician told the East Bay Express, a Bay Area weekly. "First you cause the cancer, then you profit from curing it." Both the alleged cause and cure make the GDP go up, and this syndrome has become a central dynamic of growth in the U.S. today.

Mainstream economists would argue that this is all beside the point. If people didn't have to spend money on such things as commuting or medical costs, they'd simply spend it on something else, they say. Growth would be the same or even greater, so the actual content of growth should be of little concern to those who promote it. That view holds sway in the nation's policy councils; as a result we try continually to grow our way out of problems, when increasingly we are growing our way in.

To the extent conventional economics has raised an eyebrow at growth, it has done so mainly through the concept of "externalities". These are negative side effects suffered by those not party to a transaction between a buyer and a seller. Man buys car, car pollutes air, others suffer that "externality." As the language implies, anything outside the original transaction is deemed secondary, a subordinate reality, and therefore easily overlooked. More, the effects upon buyer and seller — the "internalities" one might say — are assumed to be good.

Today however that mental schema is collapsing. Externalities are starting to overwhelm internalities. A single jet ski can cause more misery for the people who reside by a lake, than it gives pleasure to the person riding it.

More importantly, and as just discussed, internalities themselves are coming into question, and with them the assumption of choice, which is the moral linchpin of market thought.

If people choose what they buy, as market theory posits, then — externalities aside — the sum total of all their buying must be the greatest good of all. That's the ideology behind the GDP. But if people don't always choose, then the model starts to fall apart, which is what is happening today. The practical implications are obvious. If growth consists increasingly of problems rather than solutions, then scolding people for consuming too much is barking up the wrong tree. It is possible to talk instead about ridding our lives of what we don't want as well as forsaking what we do want — or think we want.

Politically this is a more promising path. But to where? The economy may be turning into a kind of round robin of difficulty and affliction, but we are all tied to the game. The sickness industry employs a lot of people, as do ad agencies and trash haulers. The fastest-growing occupations in the country include debt collectors and prison guards. What would we do without our problems and dysfunctions?

The problem is especially acute for those at the bottom of the income scale who have not shared much in the apparent prosperity. For them, a bigger piece of a bad pie might be better than none.

This is the economic conundrum of our age. No one has more than pieces of an answer, but it helps to see that much growth today is really an optical illusion created by accounting tricks. The official tally ignores totally the cost side of the growth ledger — the toll of traffic upon our time and health for example. In fact, it actually counts such costs as growth and gain. By the same token, the official tally ignores the economic contributions of the natural environment and the social structure; so that the more the economy destroys these, and puts commoditized substitutes in their places, the more the experts say the economy has "grown." Pollute the lakes and oceans so that people have to join private swim clubs and the economy grows. Erode the social infrastructure of community so people have to buy services from the market instead of getting help from their neighbors, and it grows some more. The real economy — the one that sustains us — has diminished. All that has grown is the need to buy commoditized substitutes for things we used to have for free.

So one might rephrase the question thus: how do we achieve real growth, as opposed to the statistical illusion that passes for growth today? Four decades ago, John Kenneth Galbraith argued in *The Affluent Society* that conventional economic reasoning is rapidly becoming obsolete. An economics based upon scarcity simply doesn't work in an economy of hyper-abundance, he said. If it takes a $200 billion (today) advertising industry to maintain what economists quaintly call "demand," then perhaps that demand isn't as urgent as conventional theory posits. Perhaps it's not even demand in any sane meaning of the word.

Galbraith argued that genuine economy called for shifting some resources from consumption that needs to be prodded, to needs which are indisputably great: schools, parks, older people, the inner cities and the like. For this he was skewered as a proto-socialist. Yet today the case is even stronger, as advertisers worm into virtually every waking moment in a desperate effort to keep the growth machine on track.

Galbraith was arguing for a larger public sector. But that brings dysfunctions of its own, such as bureaucracy; and it depends upon an enlarging private sector as a fiscal base to begin with. Today we need to go further, and establish new ground rules for the economy, so that it produces more genuine growth on its own. We also need to find ways to revive the nonmarket economy of informal community exchange, so that people do not need money to meet every single life need.

In the first category, environmental fiscal policy can help. While the corporate world has flogged workers to be more productive, resources such as petroleum have been in effect loafing on the job. If we used these more efficiently the result could be jobs and growth, even in conventional terms, with less environmental pollution. If we used land more efficiently — that is, reduced urban sprawl — the social and environmental gains would be great.

Another ground rule is the corporate charter laws. We need to restore these to their original purpose: to keep large business organizations within the compass of the common good. But such shifts can do only so much. More efficient cars might simply encourage more traffic, for example. Cheap renewable power for electronic devices could encourage more noise. In other words, the answer won't just be a more efficient version of what we do now. Sooner or later we'll need different ways of thinking about work and growth and how we allocate the means of life.

This is where the social economy comes in, the informal exchange between neighbors and friends. There are some promising trends. One is the return to the traditional village model in housing. Structure does affect content. When houses are close together, and people can walk to stores and work, it encourages the spontaneous social interaction that nurtures real community. New local currencies, such as Time Dollars, provide a kind of lattice work upon which informal nonmarket exchange can take root and grow.

Changes like these are off the grid of economics as conventionally defined. It took centuries for the market to emerge from the stagnation of feudalism. The next organizing principle, whatever it is, most likely will emerge slowly as well. This much we can say with certainty. As the market hurdles towards multiple implosions, social and environmental as well as financial, it is just possible that the economics profession is going to have to do what it constantly lectures the rest of us to do: adjust to new realities and show a willingness to change.

Reading number 2. The Prosperous Community: Social Capital and Public Life by Robert Putnam (American Prospect Vol 4, no 13, March 21, 1993)

Your corn is ripe today; mine will be so tomorrow. 'Tis profitable for us both, that I should labor with you today, and that you should aid me tomorrow. I have no kindness for you, and know you have as little for me. I will not, therefore, take any pains upon your account; and should I labor with you upon my own account, in expectation of a return, I know I should be disappointed, and that I should in vain depend upon your gratitude. Here then I leave you to labor alone; You treat me in the same manner. The seasons change; and both of us lose our harvests for want of mutual confidence and security.
--David Hume

The predicament of the farmers in Hume's parable is all too familiar in communities and nations around the world:

* Parents in communities everywhere want better educational opportunities for their children, but collaborative efforts to improve public schools falter.

* Residents of American ghettos share an interest in safer streets, but collective action to control crime fails.

* Poor farmers in the Third World need more effective irrigation and marketing schemes, but cooperation to these ends proves fragile.

* Global warming threatens livelihoods from Manhattan to Mauritius, but joint action to forestall this shared risk founders.

Failure to cooperate for mutual benefit does not necessarily signal ignorance or irrationality or even malevolence, as philosophers since Hobbes have underscored. Hume's farmers were not dumb, or crazy, or evil; they were trapped. Social scientists have lately analyzed this fundamental predicament in a variety of guises: the tragedy of the commons; the logic of collective action; public goods; the prisoners' dilemma. In all these situations, as in Hume's rustic anecdote, everyone would be better off if everyone could cooperate. In the absence of coordination and credible mutual commitment, however, everyone defects, ruefully but rationally, confirming one another's melancholy expectations.

How can such dilemmas of collective action be overcome, short of creating some Hobbesian Leviathan? Social scientists in several disciplines have recently suggested a novel diagnosis of this problem, a diagnosis resting on the concept of *social capital.* By analogy with notions of physical capital and human capital--tools and training that enhance individual productivity--"social capital" refers to features of social organization, such as networks, norms, and trust, that facilitate coordination and cooperation for mutual benefit. Social capital enhances the benefits of investment in physical and human capital.

Working together is easier in a community blessed with a substantial stock of social capital. This insight turns out to have powerful practical implications for many issues on the American national agenda--for how we might overcome the poverty and violence of South Central Los Angeles, or revitalize industry in the Rust Belt, or nurture the fledgling democracies of the former Soviet empire and the erstwhile Third World. Before spelling out these implications, however, let me illustrate the importance of social capital by recounting an investigation that several colleagues and I have conducted over the last two decades on the seemingly arcane subject of regional government in Italy.

LESSONS FROM AN ITALIAN EXPERIMENT

Beginning in 1970, Italians established a nationwide set of potentially powerful regional governments. These 20 new institutions were virtually identical in form, but the social, economic, political, and cultural contexts in which they were implanted differed dramatically, ranging from the preindustrial to the postindustrial, from the devoutly Catholic to the ardently Communist, from the inertly feudal to the frenetically modern. Just as a botanist might investigate plant development by measuring the growth of genetically identical seeds sown in different plots, we sought to understand government performance by studying how these new institutions evolved in their diverse settings.

As we expected, some of the new governments proved to be dismal failures--inefficient, lethargic, and corrupt. Others have been remarkably successful, however, creating innovative day care programs and job-training centers, promoting investment and economic development, pioneering environmental standards and family clinics--managing the public's business efficiently and satisfying their constituents.

What could account for these stark differences in quality of government? Some seemingly obvious answers turned out to be irrelevant. Government organization is too similar from region to region for that to explain the contrasts in performance. Party politics or ideology makes little difference. Affluence and prosperity have no direct effect. Social stability or political harmony or population movements are not the key. None of these factors is correlated with good government as we had anticipated. Instead, the best predictor is one that Alexis de Tocqueville might have expected. Strong traditions of civic engagement--voter turnout, newspaper readership, membership in choral societies and literary circles, Lions Clubs, and soccer clubs--are the hallmarks of a successful region.

Some regions of Italy, such as Emilia-Romagna and Tuscany, have many active community organizations. Citizens in these regions are engaged by public issues, not by patronage. They trust one another to act fairly and obey the law. Leaders in these communities are relatively honest and committed to equality. Social and political networks are organized horizontally, not hierarchically. These "civic communities" value solidarity, civic participation, and integrity. And here democracy works.

At the other pole are "uncivic" regions, like Calabria and Sicily, aptly characterized by the French term *incivisme*. The very concept of citizenship is stunted there. Engagement in social and cultural associations is meager. From the point of view of the inhabitants, public affairs is somebody else's business--*i notabili*, "the bosses," "the politicians"--but not theirs. Laws, almost everyone agrees, are made to be broken, but fearing others' lawlessness, everyone demands sterner discipline. Trapped in these interlocking vicious circles, nearly everyone feels powerless, exploited, and unhappy. It is hardly surprising that representative government here is less effective than in more civic communities.

The historical roots of the civic community are astonishingly deep. Enduring traditions of civic involvement and social solidarity can be traced back nearly a millennium to the eleventh century, when communal republics were established in places like Florence, Bologna, and Genoa, exactly the communities that today enjoy civic engagement and successful government. At the core of this civic heritage are rich networks of organized reciprocity and civic solidarity--guilds, religious fraternities, and tower societies for self-defense in the medieval communes; cooperatives, mutual aid societies, neighborhood associations, and choral societies in the twentieth century.

These communities did not become civic simply because they were rich. The historical record strongly suggests precisely the opposite: They have become rich because they were civic. The social capital embodied in norms and networks of civic engagement seems to be a precondition for economic development, as well as for effective government. Development economists take note: Civics matters.

How does social capital undergird good government and economic progress? First, networks of civic engagement foster sturdy norms of generalized reciprocity: I'll do this for you now, in the expectation that down the road you or someone else will return the favor. "Social capital is akin to what Tom Wolfe called the `favor bank' in his novel, *The Bonfire of the Vanities*," notes economist Robert Frank. A society that relies on generalized reciprocity is more efficient than a distrustful society, for the same reason that money is more efficient than barter. Trust lubricates social life.

Networks of civic engagement also facilitate coordination and communication and amplify information about the trustworthiness of other individuals. Students of prisoners' dilemmas and related games report that cooperation is most easily sustained through repeat play. When economic and political dealing is embedded in dense networks of social interaction, incentives for opportunism and malfeasance are reduced. This is why the diamond trade, with its extreme possibilities for fraud, is concentrated within close-knit ethnic enclaves. Dense social ties facilitate gossip and other valuable ways of cultivating reputation--an essential foundation for trust in a complex society.

Finally, networks of civic engagement embody past success at collaboration, which can serve as a cultural template for future collaboration. The civic traditions of north-central Italy provide a historical repertoire of forms of cooperation that, having proved their worth in the past, are available to citizens for addressing new problems of collective action.

Sociologist James Coleman concludes, "Like other forms of capital, social capital is productive, making possible the achievement of certain ends that would not be attainable in its absence. . . . In a farming community. . . where one farmer got his hay baled by another and where farm tools are extensively borrowed and lent, the social capital allows each farmer to get his work done with less physical capital in the form of tools and equipment." Social capital, in short, enables Hume's farmers to surmount their dilemma of collective action.

Stocks of social capital, such as trust, norms, and networks, tend to be self-reinforcing and cumulative. Successful collaboration in one endeavor builds connections and trust--social assets that facilitate future collaboration in other, unrelated tasks. As with conventional capital, those who have social capital tend to accumulate more--them as has, gets. Social capital is what the social philosopher Albert O. Hirschman calls a "moral resource," that is, a resource whose supply increases rather than decreases through use and which (unlike physical capital) becomes depleted if *not* used.

Unlike conventional capital, social capital is a "public good," that is, it is not the private property of those who benefit from it. Like other public goods, from clean air to safe streets, social capital tends to be under-provided by private agents. This means that social capital must often be a by-product of other social activities. Social capital typically consists in ties, norms, and trust transferable from one social setting to another. Members of Florentine choral societies participate because they like to sing, not because their participation strengthens the Tuscan social fabric. But it does.

SOCIAL CAPITAL AND ECONOMIC DEVELOPMENT

Social capital is coming to be seen as a vital ingredient in economic development around the world. Scores of studies of rural development have shown that a vigorous network of indigenous grassroots associations can be as essential to growth as physical investment, appropriate technology, or (that nostrum of neoclassical economists) "getting prices right." Political scientist Elinor Ostrom has explored why some cooperative efforts to manage common pool resources, like grazing grounds and water supplies, succeed, while others fail. Existing stocks of social capital are an important part of the story. Conversely, government interventions that neglect or undermine this social infrastructure can go seriously awry.

Studies of the rapidly growing economies of East Asia almost always emphasize the importance of dense social networks, so that these economies are sometimes said to represent a new brand of "network capitalism." These networks, often based on the extended family or on close-knit ethnic communities like the overseas Chinese, foster trust, lower transaction costs, and speed information and innovation. Social capital can be transmuted, so to speak, into financial capital: In novelist Amy Tan's *Joy Luck Club*, a group of mah-jong-playing friends evolves into a joint investment association. China's extraordinary economic growth over the last decade has depended less on formal institutions than on *guanxi* (personal connections) to underpin contracts and to channel savings and investment.

Social capital, we are discovering, is also important in the development of advanced Western economies. Economic sociologist Mark Granovetter has pointed out that economic transactions like contracting or job searches are more efficient when they are embedded in social networks. It is no accident that one of the pervasive stratagems of ambitious yuppies is "networking." Studies of highly efficient, highly flexible "industrial districts" (a term coined by Alfred Marshall, one of the founders of modern economics) emphasize networks of collaboration among workers and small entrepreneurs. Such concentrations of social capital, far from being paleo-industrial anachronisms, fuel ultra-modern industries from the high tech of Silicon Valley to the high fashion of Benetton. Even in mainstream economics the so-called "new growth theory" pays more attention to social structure (the "externalities of human capital") than do conventional neoclassical models. Robert Lucas, a founder of "rational expectations" economics, acknowledges that "human capital accumulation is a fundamentally *social* activity, involving *groups* of people in a way that has no counterpart in the accumulation of physical capital."

The social capital approach can help us formulate new strategies for development. For example, current proposals for strengthening market economies and democratic institutions in the formerly Communist lands of Eurasia center almost exclusively on deficiencies in financial and human capital (thus calling for loans and technical assistance). However, the deficiencies in social capital in these countries are at least as alarming. Where are the efforts to encourage "social capital formation"? Exporting PTAs or Kiwanis clubs may seem a bit far-fetched, but how about patiently reconstructing those shards of indigenous civic associations that have survived decades of totalitarian rule.

Historian S. Frederick Starr, for example, has drawn attention to important fragments of civil society--from philanthropic agencies to chess clubs--that persist from Russia's "usable past." (Such community associations provide especially valuable social capital when they cross ethnic or other cleavage lines.)

Closer to home, Bill Clinton's proposals for job-training schemes and industrial extension agencies invite attention to social capital. The objective should not be merely an assembly-line injection of booster shots of technical expertise and work-related skills into individual firms and workers. Rather, such programs could provide a matchless opportunity to create productive new linkages among community groups, schools, employers, and workers, without creating costly new bureaucracies. Why not experiment with modest subsidies for training programs that bring together firms, educational institutions, and community associations in innovative local partnerships? The latent effects of such programs on social capital accumulation could prove even more powerful than the direct effects on technical productivity.

Conversely, when considering the effects of economic reconversion on communities, we must weigh the risks of destroying social capital. Precisely because social capital is a public good, the costs of closing factories and destroying communities go beyond the personal trauma borne by individuals. Worse yet, some government programs themselves, such as urban renewal and public housing projects, have heedlessly ravaged existing social networks. The fact that these collective costs are not well measured by our current accounting schemes does not mean that they are not real. Shred enough of the social fabric and we all pay.

SOCIAL CAPITAL AND AMERICA'S ILLS

Fifty-one deaths and $1 billion dollars in property damage in Los Angeles last year put urban decay back on the American agenda. Yet if the ills are clear, the prescription is not. Even those most sympathetic to the plight of America's ghettos are not persuaded that simply reviving the social programs dismantled in the last decade or so will solve the problems. The erosion of social capital is an essential and under-appreciated part of the diagnosis.

Although most poor Americans do not reside in the inner city, there is something qualitatively different about the social and economic isolation experienced by the chronically poor blacks and Latinos who do. Joblessness, inadequate education, and poor health clearly truncate the opportunities of ghetto residents. Yet so do profound deficiencies in social capital.

Part of the problem facing blacks and Latinos in the inner city is that they lack "connections" in the most literal sense. Job-seekers in the ghetto have little access, for example, to conventional job referral networks. Labor economists Anne Case and Lawrence Katz have shown that, regardless of race, inner-city youth living in neighborhoods blessed with high levels of civic engagement are more likely to finish school, have a job, and avoid drugs and crime, controlling for the individual characteristics of the youth. That is, of two identical youths, the one unfortunate enough to live in a neighborhood whose social capital has eroded is more likely to end up hooked, booked, or dead. Several researchers seem to have found similar neighborhood effects on the incidence of teen pregnancy, among both blacks and whites, again controlling for personal characteristics. Where you live and whom you know--the social capital you can draw on--helps to define who you are and thus to determine your fate.

Racial and class inequalities in access to social capital, if properly measured, may be as great as inequalities in financial and human capital, and no less portentous. Economist Glenn Loury has used the term "social capital" to capture the fundamental fact that racial segregation, coupled with socially inherited differences in community networks and norms, means that individually targeted "equal opportunity" policies may not eliminate racial inequality, even in the long run. Research suggests that the life chances of today's generation depend not only on their parents' social resources, but also on the social resources of their parents' ethnic group. Even workplace integration and upward mobility by successful members of minority groups cannot overcome these persistent effects of inequalities in social capital. William Julius Wilson has described in tragic detail how the exodus of middle-class and working-class families from the ghetto has eroded the social capital available to those left behind. The settlement houses that nurtured sewing clubs and civic activism a century ago, embodying community as much as charity, are now mostly derelict.

It would be a dreadful mistake, of course, to overlook the repositories of social capital within America's minority communities. The neighborhood restaurant eponymously portrayed in Mitchell Duneier's recent *Slim's Table*, for example, nurtures fellowship and intercourse that enable blacks (and whites) in Chicago's South Side to sustain a modicum of collective life. Historically, the black church has been the most bounteous treasure-house of social capital for African Americans. The church provided the organizational infrastructure for political mobilization in the civil rights movement. Recent work on American political participation by political scientist Sidney Verba and his colleagues shows that the church is a uniquely powerful resource for political engagement among blacks-- an arena in which to learn about public affairs and hone political skills and make connections.

In tackling the ills of Americas cities, investments in physical capital, financial capital, human capital, and social capital are complementary, not competing alternatives. Investments in jobs and education, for example, will be more effective if they are coupled with reinvigoration of community associations.

Some churches provide job banks and serve as informal credit bureaus, for example, using their reputational capital to vouch for members who may be ex-convicts, former drug addicts, or high school dropouts. In such cases the church does not merely provide referral networks. More fundamentally, wary employers and financial institutions bank on the church's ability to identify parishioners whose formal credentials understate their reliability. At the same time, because these parishioners value their standing in the church, and because the church has put its own reputation on the line, they have an additional incentive to perform. Like conventional capital for conventional borrowers, social capital serves as a kind of collateral for men and women who are excluded from ordinary credit or labor markets. In effect, the participants pledge their social connections, leveraging social capital to improve the efficiency with which markets operate.

The importance of social capital for America's domestic agenda is not limited to minority communities. Take public education, for instance. The success of private schools is attributable, according to James Coleman's massive research, not so much to what happens in the classroom nor to the endowments of individual students, but rather to the greater engagement of parents and community members in private school activities. Educational reformers like child psychologist James Comer seek to improve schooling not merely by "treating" individual children but by deliberately involving parents and others in the educational process. Educational policymakers need to move beyond debates about curriculum and governance to consider the effects of social capital. Indeed, most commonly discussed proposals for "choice" are deeply flawed by their profoundly individualist conception of education. If states and localities are to experiment with voucher systems for education or child care, why not encourage vouchers to be spent in ways that strengthen community organization, not weaken it? Once we recognize the importance of social capital, we ought to be able to design programs that creatively combine individual choice with collective engagement.

Many people today are concerned about revitalizing American democracy. Although discussion of political reform in the United States focuses nowadays on such procedural issues as term limits and campaign financing, some of the ills that afflict the American polity reflect deeper, largely unnoticed social changes.

"Some people say that you usually can trust people. Others say that you must be wary in relations with people. Which is your view?" Responses to this question, posed repeatedly in national surveys for several decades, suggest that social trust in the United States has declined for more than a quarter century. By contrast, American politics benefited from plentiful stocks of social capital in earlier times. Recent historical work on the Progressive Era, for example, has uncovered evidence of the powerful role played by nominally non-political associations (such as women's literary societies) precisely because they provided a dense social network. Is our current predicament the result of a long-term erosion of social capital, such as community engagement and social trust?

Economist Juliet Schorr's discovery of "the unexpected decline of leisure" in America suggests that our generation is less engaged with one another outside the marketplace and thus less prepared to cooperate for shared goals. Mobile, two-career (or one-parent) families often must use the market for child care and other services formerly provided through family and neighborhood networks. Even if market-based services, considered individually, are of high quality, this deeper social trend is eroding social capital. There are more empty seats at the PTA and in church pews these days. While celebrating the productive, liberating effects of fuller equality in the workplace, we must replace the social capital that this movement has depleted.

Our political parties, once intimately coupled to the capillaries of community life, have become evanescent confections of pollsters and media consultants and independent political entrepreneurs--the very antithesis of social capital. We have too easily accepted a conception of democracy in which public policy is not the outcome of a collective deliberation about the public interest, but rather a residue of campaign strategy. The social capital approach, focusing on the indirect effects of civic norms and networks, is a much-needed corrective to an exclusive emphasis on the formal institutions of government as an explanation for our collective discontents. If we are to make our political system more responsive, especially to those who lack connections at the top, we must nourish grass-roots organization.

Classic liberal social policy is designed to enhance the opportunities of *individuals*, but if social capital is important, this emphasis is partially misplaced. Instead we must focus on community development, allowing space for religious organizations and choral societies and Little Leagues that may seem to have little to do with politics or economics. Government policies, whatever their intended effects, should be vetted for their indirect effects on social capital. If, as some suspect, social capital is fostered more by home ownership than by public or private tenancy, then we should design housing policy accordingly. Similarly, as Theda Skocpol has suggested, the direct benefits of national service programs might be dwarfed by the indirect benefits that could flow from the creation of social networks that cross class and racial lines. In any comprehensive strategy for improving the plight of America's communities, rebuilding social capital is as important as investing in human and physical capital.

Throughout the Bush administration, community self-reliance--"a thousand points of light"--too often served as an ideological fig leaf for an administration that used the thinness of our public wallet as an alibi for a lack of political will. Conservatives are right to emphasize the value of intermediary associations, but they misunderstand the potential synergy between private organization and the government. *Social capital is not a substitute for effective public policy but rather a prerequisite for it and, in part, a consequence of it.* Social capital, as our Italian study suggests, works through and with states and markets, not in place of them. The social capital approach is neither an argument for cultural determinism nor an excuse to blame the victim.

Wise policy can encourage social capital formation, and social capital itself enhances the effectiveness of government action. From agricultural extension services in the last century to tax exemptions for community organizations in this one, American government has often promoted investments in social capital, and it must renew that effort now. A new administration that is, at long last, more willing to use public power and the public purse for public purpose should not overlook the importance of social connectedness as a vital backdrop for effective policy.

Students of social capital have only begun to address some of the most important questions that this approach to public affairs suggests. What are the actual trends in different forms of civic engagement? Why do communities differ in their stocks of social capital? What *kinds* of civic engagement seem most likely to foster economic growth or community effectiveness? Must specific types of social capital be matched to different public problems? Most important of all, how is social capital created and destroyed? What strategies for building (or rebuilding) social capital are most promising? How can we balance the twin strategies of exploiting existing social capital and creating it afresh? The suggestions scattered throughout this essay are intended to challenge others to even more practical methods of encouraging new social capital formation and leveraging what we have already.

We also need to ask about the negative effects of social capital, for like human and physical capital, social capital can be put to bad purposes. Liberals have often sought to destroy some forms of social capital (from medieval guilds to neighborhood schools) in the name of individual opportunity. We have not always reckoned with the indirect social costs of our policies, but we were often right to be worried about the power of private associations. Social inequalities may be embedded in social capital. Norms and networks that serve some groups may obstruct others, particularly if the norms are discriminatory or the networks socially segregated. Recognizing the importance of social capital in sustaining community life does not exempt us from the need to worry about how that community is defined--who is inside and thus benefits from social capital, and who is outside and does not. Some forms of social capital can impair individual liberties, as critics of comunitarianism warn. Many of the Founders' fears about the "mischiefs of faction" apply to social capital. Before toting up the balance sheet for social capital in its various forms, we need to weigh costs as well as benefits. This challenge still awaits.

Progress on the urgent issues facing our country and our world requires ideas that bridge outdated ideological divides. Both liberals and conservatives agree on the importance of social empowerment, as E. J. Dionne recently noted ("The Quest for Community (Again)," *TAP*, Summer 1992). The social capital approach provides a deeper conceptual underpinning for this nominal convergence. Real progress requires not facile verbal agreement, but hard thought and ideas with high fiber content. The social capital approach promises to uncover new ways of combining private social infrastructure with public policies that work, and, in turn, of using wise public policies to revitalize America's stocks of social capital.

NOTES

NOTES

NOTES

NOTES

NOTES

NOTES

NOTES

NOTES

NOTES

NOTES